Find the Hidden Talent

Mark Powell

Legal Notice

Disclaimer

Cover Design: Mark Powell

ISBN: 9798277552360

For permissions, rights, and media inquiries, please contact:
powellmap63@gmail.com

First Edition: 2026

10 9 8 7 6 5 4 3 2 1

Table of Contents

Acknowledgments

Writing a book is never a solitary act. It may begin in silence with me staring at a blank page, but it grows only because of the voices, the faith, and the support of many people.

First, to my wife and my daughters, who have carried me through every hour of this journey. Your patience has been the quiet force behind every page, your love the anchor that kept me grounded even when my mind wandered into unfamiliar terrain. To my shadow, editor Jane Melville, this book belongs to you as much as it does to me. You are amazing.

To my friends, who reminded me that life is larger than deadlines, that laughter is as necessary to thought as discipline. I extend my gratitude to my professors at Duke University and the University of Chicago, whose teachings further opened the door to learning in psychology and neuroscience. I owe you a debt of gratitude. The foundations you laid became the scaffolding on which this work now stands.

To everyone who read my previous books, 'The Mind Beyond the Machine', 'Your Mind Beyond the Machine', and reached out with reflections, challenges, and encouragement.

Finally, a word about the process: writing this book was not a linear process. It was stop-and-start, exhilarating and exasperating. There were days when the words flowed like a raging river, and nights when I just stared at the page, convinced I had nothing left to say.

Nevertheless, during these periods, I found the book's essence and soul, demonstrating that the mind is not fixed but shaped by such moments of reflection. And when tested, it rewires itself.

To all who stood by me through this process, I thank you. This is not just my book. It is ours.

Mark Powell

SECTION I

THE PROBLEM WE DON'T SEE

Why organisations reward the wrong people

A Message to Leaders: Stop Rewarding the Wrong People

Let me speak plainly. You are probably rewarding the wrong people. I know this because I've spent almost four decades working in corporations, watching the same pattern over and over: the loudest voice becomes the leader, the boldest presentation gets the recognition and promotion, while the person who actually makes everything work quietly disappears into the background. You think you see who drives your organisation. You don't.

By the time you realise your mistake, it's often too late. Systems fracture, deadlines slip, teams demoralise, and clients start to ask questions you don't want to answer. The people who could have prevented the mess, the people who quietly hold your company together, are already halfway out the door, looking for an organisation that actually notices their worth.

Let me be blunt: ignoring hidden talent is the silent killer of organisations. Not bankruptcy. Not market shifts. Not even your competitors. It's the slow erosion of competence, continuity, and capability. Every time a quiet achiever leaves without recognition, your organisation loses months of productivity, years of accumulated knowledge, and, most importantly, the steady hands that prevent chaos from becoming catastrophe.

Here's the paradox: these people are indispensable. Yet they are invisible. They don't ask for praise. They don't send weekly self-aggrandising reports. They don't post every minor win on LinkedIn. They get the work done. And because you reward visibility over value, style over substance, and bravado over quiet brilliance, you keep promoting the wrong people, and you wonder why the organisation keeps hitting walls it shouldn't.

This book exists to change that. Finding the Hidden Talent is not about making people louder; it's about making organisations smarter. It's about teaching you, as a leader, to see the invisible, understand it, and empower it. It's about giving you the tools to spot the quiet powerhouses, to nurture them, and to structure your teams so that competence, not confidence, becomes the metric that matters.

You will find stories. Real stories from real organisations, where a single overlooked individual prevented a programme from failing, saved millions of dollars, or kept a client from walking away. You will discover psychology. Insights into what motivates these people, why they behave the way they do, and how traditional management systems fail to support them. And you will find practical tools: frameworks, checklists, and blueprints to uncover, develop, and protect your organisation's hidden engine.

I am not here to lecture. I am here to make you uncomfortable in the way that sparks action. Because action is what matters. Seeing the invisible isn't a luxury; it's survival. And in today's fast-moving, AI-infused, hyper-connected organisations, failure to recognise hidden talent is a risk you cannot afford.

So, before you turn the page, please commit, not to me, but to your organisation. Look beyond the obvious, question who is really delivering results. Pay attention to the quiet achievers in the corner. Protect them. Empower them. And if necessary, question the promotion choices, the reward systems, and the cultural biases that keep you from seeing the truth.

Your competitors are already trying to hire your hidden talent. Your systems are quietly failing in ways you don't yet understand. The future will favour organisations that can see what others overlook. And it will punish those who don't.

Because the people who save your company, who really save it, are rarely the ones you should notice. They are there. And if you learn to see them, protect them, and empower them, everything changes.

Welcome to the journey.

The Invisible Engine.

Let me tell you something most leaders never truly see. After nearly four decades navigating corporate jungles, rescuing failing programmes, dodging office politics, and watching organisations applaud the wrong people with the enthusiasm of a Wimbledon crowd celebrating a double fault, I can say this with confidence: you do not know who is really sustaining your organisation.

The people who quietly make everything work, who hold the cogs together while chaos swirls around them, are rarely the ones you reward, promote, or publicly praise. They don't dominate meetings. They don't flood inboxes. They don't perform competence; they embody it. They are invisible, silent, relentless. I call them Hidden Talent. And they are under constant threat from a powerful, deeply embedded organisational enemy: the Visibility Bias.

The Visibility Bias is the systematic tendency of organisations to conflate visibility with value. It rewards noise over substance, confidence over competence, presentation over delivery, and visibility over value. It promotes the loudest voice, the slickest slide deck, the most confidently wrong answer, while quietly exhausting the people who actually keep the system running. It doesn't look malicious, which is what makes it dangerous. It hides behind phrases like "executive presence," "leadership potential," and "strong communicator," until performance theatre becomes policy and real contribution fades into the background.

You already know these people, even if you haven't named them yet. You've felt their presence in moments of quiet crisis, when deadlines loom, systems break, and everyone else panics or disappears. They are the person who somehow understands every nuance of a system nobody else can navigate, the one who fixes problems before anyone even realises there is a problem, the miracle worker who keeps the delivery pipeline intact, clients calm, and teams sane. They don't advertise their brilliance. They don't ask for recognition. They get shit done.

I remember a programme in London in 2005 that was a mess from day one. Vendors pulled out, stakeholders argued in circles, and senior managers blamed each other with alarming efficiency. I was brought in to salvage it, assuming the problem was leadership, budget, or scope creep. I was wrong. The programme was saved by two analysts sitting quietly at the back of the room. They tracked dependencies no one else understood, rerouted workarounds, patched fragile systems, and stabilised delivery without ever raising their hands. By the end of the week, without them, the programme would have imploded. With them, it was delivered on time. No one outside that room noticed. That is Hidden Talent.

They remain invisible not because they lack impact, but because they are wired differently. Psychologically, these individuals share a rare combination of traits: a strong internal locus of control, exceptional self-regulation, a low need for external validation, high conscientiousness, an uncanny ability to recognise patterns and weak signals, and a calm that borders on suspicious when others are panicking. This makes them extraordinary contributors. It also makes them easy to miss. Organisations, for all their process and polish, still confuse visibility with value.

If you've spent more than a few minutes inside a corporate environment, you've seen how this plays out. The loudest voice is anointed the natural leader. The person with the fanciest slides gets promoted. Managing up is rewarded more than delivering out. The confidently wrong answer is praised as bold thinking. Meanwhile, the person who quietly solved the problem receives a polite "nice job" buried somewhere in a group chat, if they're lucky.

In Singapore in 2013, a critical migration project was failing. The room was full of debate, blame, and circular arguments. One junior engineer, who rarely spoke, reviewed the code, identified a misconfiguration no one else could see, and corrected it. Within hours, the migration was back on track. The room erupted in applause, but not for her. She returned to her desk, work done, largely unnoticed. That, too, is typical.

The real cost of ignoring hidden talent is not felt when people resign; it is felt long before that. It accumulates quietly. Their ideas are dismissed. Their competence is taken for granted. Their boundaries are tested because they are dependable. Someone louder takes credit for their work. They are expected to fix everything and are rewarded with nothing. By the time they leave, they are already mentally halfway out the door, searching for jobs that don't involve saving incompetent people. When they go, the loss is not just emotional. It encompasses financial, operational, and strategic factors: recruitment costs, onboarding time, knowledge loss, delivery failures, morale erosion, client dissatisfaction, and strategic drift. The spreadsheet of pain is endless.

Hidden talent is not merely a corporate asset; it is the heartbeat of your organisation. These people make the impossible look ordinary. They solve problems you didn't even know existed. They are the quiet architects of stability, continuity, and progress. Without them, systems fracture, clients suffer, and ambitions unravel. And yet most organisations continue to reward visibility over value, noise over substance, bravado over quiet genius.

I have lost count of how many times I have seen a project teeter on the edge. At the same time, leadership debates style over substance, while a calm, competent individual at the back quietly fixes the workflow, rewrites a critical script, or realigns a team. No fanfare. No acknowledgement. Everything works again. That is the paradox of hidden talent: indispensable, yet invisible.

This matters now more than ever. Organisations no longer want bigger teams; they want smarter ones. Leaner operations. Faster delivery. People who can think, not just perform. People who can work with AI rather than panic at it. Leaders who can see what truly drives performance. The absolute goldmine is already inside your organisation. Hidden talent is your unrealised competitive advantage. Uncover them, empower them, protect them, and your organisation transforms from a reactive, noisy machine into a disciplined, intelligent system capable of extraordinary things. Ignore them, and you will spend the subsequent decade firefighting recruitment crises, delivery failures, and morale collapse.

Finding hidden talent requires a shift in how leaders see. You must learn to recognise competence without fanfare, potential without presentation, contribution without applause. You must notice the quiet patterns of behaviour: the people who fix things before meetings start, who stay calm when others panic, who see what others miss. These are the people who hold your organisation together. Psychologically, they thrive in environments that respect autonomy and competence. They are intrinsically motivated. They do not need spectacle or constant validation. They flourish when trusted and wither in cultures that prioritise appearance over substance.

In Singapore in 2017, during a regulatory banking programme on the verge of failure, one quiet project manager reorganised the entire workflow into a single spreadsheet. No announcement. No presentation. Just clarity, precision, and execution. That spreadsheet served as the foundation for the regulatory submission. The risk evaporated. The hero remained invisible.

I have spent thirty years being called when things go wrong. Every time, the pattern is the same: a handful of brilliant, quiet, psychologically fascinating humans hold everything together, while organisations focus their attention on the loudest, most confident, and often least competent voices in the room. This book is my attempt to change that. It is practical, candid, and deeply psychological. It is not about making people louder; it is about making organisations smarter. It is not about charisma; it is about competence. It is about learning to see the value that has always been there, quietly sustaining everything.

When hidden talent is recognised, supported, and protected, organisations do not merely survive; they thrive. Delivery improves. Innovation accelerates. Morale rises. Stability becomes a given, not a hope. Leadership becomes grounded in substance rather than performance. And most importantly, the people who make it all possible are finally seen.

So, the next time a programme fails, a system breaks, or a client escalates, look beyond the obvious. Look for the quiet achievers. The ones who do not announce their accomplishments. The ones who do not seek recognition. The ones who quietly and consistently make everything work. They are your hidden talent. They are your invisible engine. And they are your future.

This is Finding the Hidden Talent.

The People You Promoted Instead

Most leaders can recall the moment a promotion decision felt right. The meeting ends, and a consensus forms. The rationale sounds solid. The chosen candidate speaks well, presents confidently, and looks the part. There is relief in the room. Decision made. Box ticked. Momentum preserved.

And for a while, everything seems fine.

Then the cracks appear. Not dramatically. Quietly. Delivery slows. Problems escalate instead of disappearing. Meetings multiply. The team compensates. Dependable people stay late. The newly promoted leader delegates upward rather than downward. Eventually, someone senior asks the question no one wants to answer: Why does this feel harder than it should?

If this sounds familiar, this chapter is for you.

Because here is a truth many organisations avoid: a large proportion of leadership problems are not caused by talent shortages, but by promotion mistakes. Not random mistakes. Predictable ones. Repeated ones. Systemic ones.

This is where the Visibility Bias does its most damage.

Most promotions are not decisions about capability. They are decisions about confidence signals. We promote people who speak fluently in power rooms. People who sound decisive under pressure. People who narrate complexity convincingly, even when they struggle to manage it. We tell ourselves we are rewarding potential, when in reality we are rewarding familiarity, comfort, and presentation skill. Every time we do this, someone else pays the price. And that someone is rarely the person promoted.

It is the quiet high-performer who must now compensate for them.

Let me describe three people you have almost certainly promoted.

The first is the Articulate Improviser. This person is verbally fluent, quick-thinking, and confident. They can answer almost any question, often persuasively, occasionally incorrectly, but always convincingly. In interviews, they shine. In meetings, they dominate. They think out loud, which sounds like leadership. They are comfortable with ambiguity, which is mistaken for strategic depth. When things go wrong, they explain convincingly why it was unavoidable.

What they are often less good at is follow-through. Depth. Sustained execution. Their confidence masks blind spots. Their teams expend considerable effort translating vision into reality, correcting misjudgments, and revising decisions made too quickly. The leader looks effective. The system quietly absorbs the cost.

The second is the Dependable Performer. This one feels safe. They have been around a long time. They know how things work. They rarely cause problems. They manage well. When promoted, nothing breaks. But nothing grows either. Delivery plateaus. Innovation slows. Capability quietly drains away. This is leadership by inertia, steady, comfortable, and ultimately limiting.

The third is the Charismatic Protector. This person is liked. Often deeply liked. They advocate for their team, speak passionately about culture, and present as caring and engaged. What is less visible is how much of the team's success is actually driven by one or two quiet individuals beneath the narrative. When those individuals leave, the charisma remains, but the results don't.

Pause here.

If you are instinctively defending any of these people, that's normal. They are not villains. Most are capable, well-intentioned professionals. That is precisely why this pattern is so dangerous. The problem is not promoting bad people. The problem is that it promotes the wrong signal.

Because somewhere near each of those promotion decisions, there was someone else.

Someone quieter. Someone less fluent. Someone who didn't self-nominate. Someone who solved problems before they escalated. Someone who made delivery feel boring because nothing ever went wrong. Someone who didn't interview well because they didn't perform competently, but they practised it.

You didn't promote them.

And you probably had reasons.

"They're not visible enough."

"They're brilliant, but not leadership material."

"They don't speak up."

"They don't seem ambitious."

These phrases sound responsible. They feel measured. They are also the language of the Visibility Bias.

What you were really saying was: They don't look like what we reward.

Here is where the "oh shit" moment usually lands.

Think back to a promotion that didn't quite work. Not a disaster, just a slow bleed. Think about who became busier as a result. Who stayed late? Who fixed things that shouldn't have needed fixing? Who stopped offering ideas? Who quietly disengaged.

That person didn't fail your organisation.

Your organisation failed them.

The cost didn't appear immediately. It never does. It shows up later as burnout, attrition, disengagement, and a creeping sense that things feel heavier than they used to.

I have observed this pattern across industries, geographies, and cultures: banking, technology, healthcare, government, start-ups, and multinationals. The faces change. The dynamic does not.

The most dangerous moment in any organisation is when leadership mistakes confidence for capacity. When storytelling outruns systems thinking. When the ability to speak replaces the ability to see.

This becomes acute under pressure. Tight timelines. High scrutiny. Complex environments. Leaders reach for familiarity. They promote individuals who make them feel safe in meetings, people who reassure rather than resolve, who manage perception rather than reality.

Meanwhile, the people who actually stabilise the system are implicitly told that what they bring is not leadership. It is "support."

Hidden talent hears that message clearly.

They learn that solving problems quietly is less valuable than narrating them loudly. That reliability is expected but not rewarded. That credit flows upward and outward, rarely downward. They begin to adjust. Not dramatically. Subtly. They stop volunteering ideas. They stop correcting mistakes publicly. They disengage just enough to protect themselves.

And you don't notice.

Because the system still works, for a while.

This is the paradox leaders often miss: hidden talent makes poor leadership look functional. Their competence masks organisational weakness. Their resilience absorbs bad decisions. Their commitment fills gaps no one sees. They are the reason many organisations survive leadership mistakes far longer than they should.

Until they don't.

I once worked with an organisation that could not understand why delivery kept slipping despite "strong leadership appointments." On paper, everything was right. Competency frameworks. Rigorous interviews. Positive feedback. What the data didn't capture was that three senior engineers, the people who had historically prevented crises, had quietly disengaged. They still showed up. They still delivered. They stopped compensating. And suddenly everything broke at once.

Leadership blamed complexity. The market. The pace of change. They never asked the most critical question: Who stopped carrying the load?

This is why exit interviews are such a blunt instrument. By the time someone leaves, the damage is already done. The absolute failure happened years earlier, in a meeting where someone else got the job.

Here is the most brutal truth in this chapter: if you are a leader, you have almost certainly rewarded the wrong person at least once, not because you are careless, but because the system trained you to.

The Visibility Bias is not a personal flaw. It is an organisational reflex. It thrives in cultures that equate speaking with thinking, motion with progress, and presence with value.

It creates a closed loop: the more visible you are, the more valuable you appear; the more valuable you appear, the more authority you gain; the more authority you gain, the easier it is to remain visible, regardless of what is actually accomplished.

Hidden talent cannot compete in that economy. Nor should they have to.

Some readers will feel defensive here. Others will feel uncomfortable. A few will feel relieved because something they have sensed for years finally has a name. All of those reactions are valid. This chapter is not about blame. It is about responsibility.

Because once you see this pattern, you cannot unsee it.

You begin to notice who speaks first and who finishes tasks. Who narrates success and who engineers it. Who absorbs risk and who distributes it. You start to see meetings differently. Promotions differently. "High-potential" lists differently.

You may even recognise people you unintentionally sidelined.

That recognition can sting.

Sit with it.

Leaders who build extraordinary organisations do not make mistakes. They are the ones willing to confront the invisible.

If you can honestly ask yourself, Who did I promote instead? You are already ahead of most. If you can name the quiet person who paid the price for that decision, you are closer still.

The chapters that follow will give you tools and frameworks to correct this, to identify hidden talent, protect it, and build systems that reward value over noise. But none of that matters if you skip this moment.

This is the point where leadership becomes a choice rather than a title.

Because the future of your organisation will not be decided by who speaks best in rooms of power, it will be decided by who quietly ensures that things work when no one is watching.

The question is no longer whether hidden talent exists.

The question is whether you are willing to see the people you promoted instead and decide differently next time.

Who's Actually Doing the Work

Psychologically, this is how you find those hidden diamonds in the mounds of coal. The ones who don't push to be seen, who don't strut or shout, but who quietly carry brilliance like it's a private inheritance. If you want to understand how to identify hidden talent, the real engines of performance, you need to understand not just behaviour, but the science beneath it. Because competence doesn't behave like noise, it behaves like gravity. You don't always notice it, but everything depends on it.

Hidden talent exists everywhere in your organisation, like constellations you only notice when the sky turns dark. If you don't know what you're looking for, you'll miss them entirely. They won't introduce themselves. They won't wave CVs in your face or send late-night emails purely to be seen. They don't curate a personal brand or a LinkedIn persona. They proceed, which is why traditional systems overlook them. Traditional systems favour self-promotion. But psychology favours substance. And substance, when you understand it, has patterns.

The first thing to grasp is this: the people who deliver the most are often the least interested in broadcasting their worth. There's a psychological principle behind this called the Dunning-Kruger inverse. We tend to speak loudest about the things we understand the least. Those who barely know what they're doing frequently ooze confidence because they lack the self-awareness to recognise their gaps. Meanwhile, the highly competent underestimate themselves because they're keenly aware of complexity. They don't assume expertise; they earn it, examine it, and question it. So, ironically, the more someone truly knows, the less likely they are to shout about it. Hidden talent is hidden partly because it's humble.

You see this everywhere. The best engineers are the ones who phrase solutions like, "Well… It's not perfect, but this might work." The best analysts say things like, "I may be wrong, but the data suggests…" The best problem-solvers are the ones who follow up a heroic rescue with, "It wasn't a big deal." They are chronically allergic to grandstanding. Their competence is internal; their ego is quiet. They want to be accurate, not applauded. When you understand this psychological signature, it becomes easier to identify.

Another principle comes from cognitive load theory. People with high competence expend less mental energy on complex work. They move through tasks with an ease others misinterpret as "not doing much." Leaders assume that the person who's frantic and breathless is more invested than the person who completes the same task calmly and predictably. The science says the opposite. Efficiency looks calm. Mastery looks. Quiet productivity masks a roaring intellect.

So how do you find them? You look for consistency over theatrics. You look for patterns of steady output. You look for the person whose work quality doesn't fluctuate with their mood. You look for the individual everyone instinctively turns to when things go wrong, not because they're loud, but because they're reliable. Hidden talent has a gravitational pull. People trust them, even when the organisation hasn't noticed why. Pay attention to where others naturally gravitate, and you'll find the quiet anchors of your organisation.

There's also a neuropsychological factor at play. Some people's brains are wired for depth rather than display. Their default mode network is more active, indicating they spend more time reflecting, integrating, and thinking more deeply. These are the people who contribute in ways that aren't immediately visible but are undeniably impactful. They don't react impulsively. They synthesise. Their brains literally process work differently. They think in layers rather than in bursts. They favour long-term outcomes over short-term applause. If you want to spot them, look for depth disguised as quietness.

Emotionally, hidden talent shows up in another interesting way: they have a low need for external validation. Psychologists call this intrinsic motivation. They do the work because the work matters to them. They don't need applause; they need purpose. They don't require the dopamine hit of being seen. They generate dopamine internally through progress, craftsmanship, and problem-solving. This makes them extraordinarily powerful in any team, because performance optics does not drive them. They're driven by meaning. Meaning fosters resilience, longevity, and genuine excellence.

In contrast, noisy performers often need constant reinforcement. Their motivation is extrinsic. Without visibility, their fuel runs out. Hidden talent only needs trust. That difference, once you spot it, changes everything.

Let me introduce a tool here, a little secret you can carry in your mind and your notebook. I call it the Quiet Value Formula (QVF). It's deceptively simple, but it cuts through all the noise, office politics, and performative busyness that so often masks actual competence. Hidden talent isn't flashy. It doesn't advertise itself. It quietly delivers results, day in, day out. The QVF is a way to measure that hidden brilliance without relying on visibility, charisma, or the endless parade of status updates that so often distract leaders from what actually matters.

Here's the formula:

QVF = (Consistency × Competence) ÷ Noise

Let's break it down.

Consistency is how reliably a person delivers. Hidden talent doesn't appear brilliant once a month; it shows up, steady and dependable, every day, week after week. Competence is the quality and depth of their output, their ability to solve complex problems, create meaningful solutions, and lift the standard of everyone around them. And Noise is how much attention-seeking behaviour they exhibit, emails sent to be noticed, meetings hijacked for self-promotion, reports rewritten in glittering slides rather than substance. The higher the QVF, the more likely you are to be looking at someone who quietly carries your organisation forward. A low QVF? That's the person who's loud but leaves little behind, often confusing motion with impact.

The beauty of this formula is twofold. First, it makes invisible contributions visible. Second, it's actionable. When you evaluate your team using QVF, you begin to observe patterns. You notice the people whose calm, steady competence prevents crises. You see the ones who solve problems without asking for a parade. You notice the quiet anchors your organisation can't function without. And the more you look, the clearer it becomes that real value rarely screams; it whispers, it nudges, it quietly accumulates over time.

The QVF isn't just a formula; it's a lens. It trains your mind to notice the people who actually matter, the ones who sustain productivity, culture, and innovation from behind the scenes. Use it, and you'll stop rewarding noise just because it's loud. You'll start recognising the diamonds in the rough. You'll learn to invest in the people who silently deliver, and in doing so, you'll build teams that thrive, not in appearances, but in reality. Ultimately, organisations operate on competence, not applause. The QVF shows exactly where that competence resides.

If you want to spot hidden talent, you also need to pay attention to peer behaviour long before metrics surface. Who do colleagues instinctively turn to when stuck? Who do they rely on when something breaks? Peer selection is one of the strongest, most reliable indicators of competence. Teams always know who their quiet backbone is long before leadership does. Hidden talent carries social gravity; it elevates the group without ever seeking credit. They stabilise a team's nervous system, reducing anxiety, preventing errors, and keeping projects on track without dramatic flair.

Behaviourally, hidden talent exhibits what psychologists call response latency; they pause before answering, not because they're indecisive, but because they're thinking deeply. Their pauses signal cognitive processing, not uncertainty. Contrast that with loud performers, who often respond instantly, speaking to dominate rather than solve. Hidden talent thinks first, acts second, and typically leaves a trail of high-quality outcomes that others notice only in retrospect.

Neuropsychology gives us further insight. People who quietly excel often demonstrate a stronger default mode network, higher intrinsic motivation, and exceptional emotional regulation. They treat repetition not as monotony but as craft. They tolerate delayed gratification. They thrive in complexity, uncertainty, and long-term projects, conditions that often frustrate the attention-seeking performers. When chaos hits, they adapt. When pressure mounts, they focus. They reduce cognitive load on the system rather than increase it.

Hidden talent also carries what I like to call the competence ceiling paradox: the more skilled they become, the more acutely aware they are of what they don't know. This humility isn't self-doubt; it's sophistication. It makes them perpetual learners, constantly refining, improving, and elevating standards without ever demanding applause. Their curiosity, precision, and intrinsic drive are quietly contagious; they lift the performance of everyone around them without requiring them to perform themselves.

In practice, spotting these individuals requires observation beyond surface metrics. Look for patterns over time, not headlines. Notice calm in the face of chaos. Notice those who solve problems rather than announce them. Notice where colleagues naturally gravitate in high-pressure moments. Notice who quietly improves the work of others without fanfare. Apply the QVF mentally: weigh consistency, competence, and noise. Over time, patterns emerge, and the hidden talent becomes visible, not because they changed, but because you finally learned how to see them.

Ultimately, hidden talent doesn't need a spotlight to matter. But for your organisation to survive and thrive, you must recognise it, trust it, and protect it. Leaders who fail to do so end up with a team full of noise and little substance. Leaders who succeed cultivate environments where quiet competence is amplified, valued, and invested in. And those leaders will watch as their hidden diamonds quietly but relentlessly transform their teams, their culture, and their results into something remarkable.

Because organisations may run on noise temporarily, but they survive and excel on competence. The people who quietly deliver are not just valuable; they are indispensable. And with the Quiet Value Formula, you finally have a way to see them clearly, measure them meaningfully, and give them the recognition they've quietly earned all along.

Why Noise Keeps Winning

There is also a structural reason noise persists that leaders rarely acknowledge, because it sits uncomfortably close to power. Noise is easier to manage than value. It is easier to respond to someone who is constantly present than to someone who is consistently effective but rarely visible. Presence creates a sense of familiarity, and familiarity is often mistaken for trust.

Trust, however, is built on outcomes, not airtime.

In many organisations, leaders are rewarded for decisiveness, speed, and confidence. These traits are not inherently flawed, but they create an environment in which thinking aloud is conflated with feeling well. The leader who fills the silence appears in control. The one who pauses seems uncertain. Over time, silence itself becomes suspect.

Quiet contributors feel this shift acutely. They sense that reflection is interpreted as hesitation. That careful thinking is interpreted as risk. That nuance is unwelcome when certainty is demanded. Rather than forcing themselves into a posture that feels false, they withdraw further into the work itself.

This is not disengagement. It is misalignment.

Another reason noise survives is that it distributes responsibility thinly. When many voices speak, accountability blurs. Meetings end with action items assigned broadly rather than owned deeply.

The appearance of collective effort masks the absence of individual ownership. Quiet talent often becomes the anchor that compensates for this diffusion, stepping in to ensure things actually happen.

Ironically, the more noise increases, the greater the pressure on the quiet ones.

They become the default problem solvers, not because they seek it, but because they are dependable. They pick up dropped threads. They close loops no one else noticed were open. Over time, this becomes expected rather than appreciated. Reliability turns into an obligation.

This is one of the most corrosive dynamics in modern organisations. The people least likely to demand recognition are often given the most responsibility. Those most comfortable with effort are often given the least accountability. The system rewards expression over execution, while quietly taxing those who deliver.

From the outside, this is a functioning organisation. From the inside, it feels unbalanced.

Leaders often defend this by pointing to effort. Everyone seems busy. Calendars are full. Messages are constant. The problem is that busyness has become a substitute for effectiveness. People optimise for appearing indispensable rather than being useful.

The quiet contributors do not play this game well because the game itself feels pointless to them. They care about resolution, not recognition. They want problems solved, not discussed endlessly. They measure success by stability rather than applause.

And so, they endure.

They endure meetings that add little value. They endure decisions made without sufficient context. They endure the frustration of watching loud contributors take credit for work they quietly completed. Each instance feels minor, but together they accumulate into something heavier.

What is often misunderstood is that quiet talent does not leave solely because of workload. They leave because of moral exhaustion. The exhaustion of seeing effort decoupled from reward. The exhaustion of knowing what matters but being unable to influence how it is valued.

Before they leave, they adapt.

They stop correcting others publicly. They stop offering suggestions that will be ignored. They stop volunteering for work that will only increase their load. They narrow their contribution to what is explicitly required. This is not disengagement in the traditional sense. It is self-protection.

From a leadership perspective, this stage is almost invisible. Performance remains acceptable. Behaviour remains professional. Nothing appears wrong.

Until it is.

When the quiet ones finally exit, leaders often discover that the organisation was far more dependent on them than anyone realised. Knowledge gaps emerge. Dependencies surface. Things that used to work no longer do. The noise continues, but outcomes deteriorate.

This is when organisations experience what appears to be sudden fragility. In reality, the fragility was always there. People were holding it together; no one was paying attention to it.

Another uncomfortable truth is that noise is often mistaken for leadership potential. People who speak confidently, dominate discussions, and frame narratives are seen as future leaders, even when their track record of delivery is thin. Meanwhile, those who consistently execute are seen as strong contributors rather than leaders.

This creates a pipeline problem. Organisations promote those skilled at performance into roles that require judgement, while keeping those with judgement in roles that lack influence. Over time, decision quality declines even as communication increases.

Leaders then wonder why execution feels harder than it used to.

The answer is rarely capability. It is a misplacement.

There is also a cultural dimension that reinforces noise. Many organisations claim to value collaboration, but what they actually reward is participation. Speaking up is equated with engagement. Silence is equated with passivity. This ignores the fact that some of the most collaborative individuals contribute through action rather than commentary.

Quiet talent collaborates by making things work.

They build bridges informally. They share knowledge quietly. They support others without announcing it. This form of collaboration is more complex to measure, but far more impactful. When organisations fail to recognise it, they inadvertently discourage it.

This leads to a paradox. The more organisations talk about teamwork, the less effective their teams become, because the performance of togetherness drowns out coordinated work.

To change this, leaders must become literate in a different language of contribution. One that values follow-through over follow-up. Resolution over rhetoric. Substance over show.

This requires leaders to slow down their own behaviour. To speak less and listen more. To notice who improves outcomes even when no one is watching. To ask who made the difference, not who explained the difference.

It also requires courage. The courage to challenge the assumption that confidence equals capability. The courage to reward people who do not fit the traditional leadership mould. The courage to tolerate quieter rooms in exchange for stronger results.

Organisations that make this shift experience a subtle but profound transformation. Meetings become shorter and more focused. Decisions become fewer but better. People feel less pressure to perform and more freedom to think. Quiet contributors re-engage, not because they are suddenly visible, but because they are finally valued.

Noise does not disappear in these environments. It simply loses its advantage.

When noise no longer guarantees reward, value begins to emerge naturally.

This is how cultures change. Not through slogans or initiatives, but through what leaders notice, protect, and reward. When leaders learn to see past noise, they uncover a depth of capability that was always there, waiting patiently beneath the surface.

Quiet competence has never been the problem.
The problem has always been our willingness to listen for it.

SECTION II

RISK AND CONSEQUENCE

What happens when hidden talent is ignored

The Risk You Never Saw Coming

Most organisational failures don't begin with chaos. They begin with things feeling *fine*.

Projects are delivered. Meetings run on time. Dashboards glow reassuringly green. Nothing appears sufficiently broken to warrant concern. And that is precisely when the real risk starts to form.

I call this the 'Watermelon effect': Green on the outside, Red inside.

It doesn't announce itself in meetings. It doesn't trigger alarms. It accumulates quietly, disguised as stability.

What makes this risk so dangerous is that it doesn't look like a risk at all. It seems like competence. It feels calm. It presents itself as control.

In most organisations, huge ones, leaders are trained to look for disruption and missed deadlines. Budget overruns. Escalations. Complaints. These are the signals that trigger attention. But hidden talent failures do not begin with disruption. They start with accommodation.

Someone compensates. Someone stays late. Someone fixes the issue quietly rather than raising it. Someone absorbs the friction, so the system continues to appear smooth. From the outside, everything looks fine. Internally, the load is being redistributed in ways no one is tracking.

This is how fragility grows under the appearance of strength.

In the early stages, leaders often sense that something is off, but they struggle to articulate it. Meetings feel heavier. Decisions take slightly longer. Questions arise that should not need to be asked. But because outcomes are still being delivered, these signals are dismissed as noise. Pressure. Complexity. The cost of doing business at scale.

This is the first rationalisation.

We tell ourselves that the system is under strain because the environment is challenging, not because the system itself is becoming brittle. We attribute discomfort to external forces rather than internal imbalance. After all, the numbers still look acceptable. The milestones are still being reported as achieved. Clients have not complained. Regulators have not intervened.

Nothing has changed, we say.

What has actually changed is that the margin for error has disappeared.

Hidden talent often functions as that margin. They are the ones who catch inconsistencies before they compound. They notice patterns others miss. They can anticipate when a decision that appears correct on paper will fail in practice. When they are fully engaged, the organisation benefits from their judgement without ever acknowledging it.

When they begin to disengage, the organisation continues to operate, but without the safety net it once had.

This is where leaders make their second rationalisation. They assume that because things are still working, the people involved must still be fine. Silence is interpreted as stability. Reliability is interpreted as resilience. The absence of complaint is mistaken for contentment.

In reality, something more subtle is happening.

Hidden talent rarely confronts leadership directly. They are not wired for confrontation. They are wired for responsibility. When they feel unseen or taken for granted, they do not protest. They adapt. They reduce scope. They stop offering early warnings. They focus narrowly on what they are accountable for and let the rest surface naturally.

From a governance perspective, this looks healthy. Issues are being raised through formal channels. Escalations are being logged. Risks are being documented. Leaders feel reassured that transparency has improved.

What they do not realise is that the system has lost its informal immune response.

The slow burn continues.

Minor issues that would once have been resolved quietly now require meetings. Decisions that would once have been made with confidence now require alignment. Work that would once have flowed now encounters friction. Leaders respond by adding structure. More checkpoints. More reporting. More oversight.

This is the third rationalisation. We believe we are increasing control when, in fact, we are compensating for the loss of judgment.

At this point, the organisation becomes busier without becoming more effective. People attend more meetings but leave with less clarity. Work expands to fill the space created by uncertainty. The noise level increases, but the underlying capability remains unchanged.

Still, there is no crisis.

This is why the risk remains unseen. Leaders are trained to respond to events, not to erosion.

I have watched organisations operate in this state for months, sometimes years. From the outside, they appear successful. From the inside, those carrying the load feel increasingly alone. They are still competent. Still professional. Still delivering. But the cost is rising.

Eventually, something gives.

It is rarely the thing leaders expect.

Sometimes it is a departure that seems inexplicable. A resignation that comes without warning. The explanation is vague. A new opportunity. A change of direction. A desire for balance. Leaders are surprised but not alarmed. After all, turnover happens.

Sometimes a small failure triggers a disproportionate response. A report was submitted late. A control was missed. A dependency overlooked. On its own, it should not matter. But because the system is already stretched, the impact cascades. What should have been a minor issue becomes a significant problem.

This is the moment leaders often describe later as the point where everything suddenly changed.

In truth, nothing changed in that moment. Everything had already changed. The organisation ran out of slack.

Perceived control gives way to revealed fragility.

The reason this feels so shocking is that leaders believed they were managing risk effectively. They had visibility. They had dashboards. They had governance. What they lacked was insight into who was quietly holding things together.

This is why the Carol moment matters.

It is not about one individual. It is about what she represents. She was not an outlier. She was a pattern—a pattern that exists in almost every organisation, operating below the threshold of recognition.

The danger is not that leaders fail to reward people like Carol. The danger is that they build systems that depend on people like Carol without ever acknowledging that dependence.

When those systems are stressed, the costs become apparent, but by then, it is too late to respond effectively.

I have seen leaders react to this realisation with a mix of regret and urgency. They want to fix things quickly. They introduce recognition programmes. They hold town halls. They talk about values. These actions are well-intentioned, but they often miss the point.

The issue was never a lack of appreciation. It was a lack of attention.

Hidden talent does not need applause. It requires leaders to identify where the real work is occurring and to design systems that do not punish those who do it quietly.

The risk you did not anticipate is not a single failure. It is the gradual misalignment between those who create value and those who receive recognition. Between who carries the risk and who is rewarded for managing its appearance.

When that misalignment persists, organisations become fragile even as they appear strong.

The lesson from that $400 million programme was not that Carol deserved more praise, although she did. It was that the organisation had unknowingly entrusted its financial integrity to someone it barely recognised.

That is not resilience. That is luck.

Leadership is often described as the art of seeing around corners. In reality, it is the discipline of seeing what is already there.

The most serious risks facing organisations today are not always external. They are embedded in how work is distributed, how effort is absorbed, and how value is perceived. Until leaders recognise those dynamics, they will continue to be surprised by outcomes they believe came from nowhere.

Nothing changed, until everything did.

By then, the cost was already fixed.

When Hidden Talent Breaks

Hidden talent rarely fails loudly.

That is one of the reasons organisations misunderstand what is happening when things begin to go wrong. Failure, in most leadership narratives, is dramatic. A missed deadline. A public incident. A visible collapse. A sudden resignation that triggers panic. Hidden talent does not operate this way; when it breaks, leaders often misinterpret the signs or miss them entirely.

What actually happens is quieter, slower, and far more dangerous.

Hidden talent breaks long before it leaves.

I have seen this pattern repeat across industries, geographies, and organisational cultures. The individuals who possess the most profound operational understanding, who stabilise systems under pressure, and who catch problems before they escalate do not suddenly stop caring. They do not abruptly disengage. They do not make a scene. They begin by narrowing their contribution.

At first, it appears to be nothing.

They stop volunteering ideas. They answer only what is asked. They reduce discretionary effort. They stop anticipating problems and focus only on their immediate remit. The work still gets done, but the invisible safety margin begins to shrink. Leaders do not notice this because the visible outputs remain intact.

This is the most dangerous phase because the organisation is still functioning, and leadership assumes that all is well.

Hidden talent does not break because of a single event. It breaks because of accumulation. Small moments of being overlooked. Repeated instances where visible performance is praised while invisible effort is assumed. Decisions taken without consultation. Credit given to those who narrate rather than those who build.

None of these moments, in isolation, feels catastrophic. But together they send a message that is unmistakable to those who are paying attention. What you do matters less than how it is seen.

Hidden talent hears this message early.

There is a second phase that often follows. Quiet withdrawal.

This is where leaders begin to notice that something is different, but they struggle to articulate what it is. Responses become shorter. Engagement in meetings has reduced. The person remains reliable, competent, and professional, but something has shifted. They are no longer emotionally invested in the outcome, only in the task.

Leaders often misinterpret this phase. They assume the individual is content, stable, perhaps even loyal. Silence is mistaken for satisfaction. Reliability is mistaken for resilience.

In reality, the individual is conserving energy.

Hidden talent is often deeply conscientious. When they feel taken for granted, they do not rebel. They protect themselves. They reduce exposure. They stop carrying the risk that no one sees. They begin to ask a quiet question that determines everything that follows.

Is this still worth it?

The third phase is the one organisations remember, because it finally becomes visible. Departure.

When hidden talent leaves, it often appears sudden. There is shock. Confusion. Leaders ask how this could have happened without warning. They review exit interviews and are surprised by the calmness of the explanation. Better opportunity. New challenge. Time for a change.

What is rarely acknowledged is that the real departure happened months, sometimes years earlier. The physical exit is only the final step.

The cost of this kind of loss is not captured in standard metrics. It does not show up neatly in attrition dashboards or engagement surveys. What disappears is institutional memory, informal influence, and the quiet judgment that prevents minor issues from becoming big ones.

I have seen organisations spend months, sometimes years, trying to replace someone whose job title did not reflect their actual value. Multiple hires fail to replicate the impact. Documentation exists, but context does not. Processes are followed, but outcomes degrade. People begin to say things like "it used to work" or "we never had this problem before."

That is the moment leaders realise something fundamental has changed.

There is another failure mode that is even harder to detect. Hidden talent remains, but no longer protects the system.

This is not malicious. It is human. When people feel unseen, they stop absorbing pain on behalf of the organisation. They allow issues to surface rather than intercepting them. They escalate rather than resolve quietly. They do not bend the rules to keep things moving. They operate strictly within their defined role.

From a governance perspective, this looks healthy. From a performance perspective, it is devastating.

For leaders, this results in an increase in visible problems. More escalations. More meetings. More oversight. More controls. The organisation becomes noisier, not because people are working harder, but because the quiet work that kept things smooth has stopped.

Leaders respond by adding structure, process, and reporting. They attempt to manage what they can now see. But what they have lost is the invisible layer that made the visible layer effective.

Hidden talent breaking is not an emotional story. It is a systems story.

It is about load, trust, and reciprocity. When individuals consistently give more than they receive in recognition, autonomy, or respect, something eventually gives. Not explosively, but incrementally.

This is why prevention matters more than recovery.

Once hidden talent has disengaged, it is challenging to reattach them fully. Praise feels late. Attention feels performative. Invitations feel transactional. The trust that allowed quiet contributions to flourish has been eroded.

Leaders often ask what they could have done differently. The answer is rarely complex.

They could have noticed earlier.
They could have asked better questions.
They could have recognised the contribution before it became an absence.

This chapter exists to make one thing clear. Hidden talent breaking is not an anomaly. It is a predictable outcome of systems that reward noise over substance.

If you want to protect your organisation, you must protect the people who defend it without being asked.

If you wait until they break, you will already be too late.

Hidden Talent Economics: The Cost of Ignoring the Invisible Engine

Let us go one layer deeper, because the economics of hidden talent are not only about loss. They are about distortion.

When organisations fail to recognise invisible contributions, they do not simply lose value. They misallocate it. Resources flow towards what is seen rather than what sustains. Investment follows narrative rather than necessity. Over time, this creates a dangerous illusion of efficiency. The organisation appears busy, active, and productive. In reality, it is being quietly propped up by a shrinking group of people whose effort is never properly accounted for.

This is where many leaders get trapped. They believe they are optimising performance because all the visible indicators look healthy. Projects appear to be on track. Risks appear to be managed. Clients appear satisfied. What they do not see is the human buffering occurring beneath the surface. Extra hours absorbed without complaint. Judgement calls made without escalation. Errors are intercepted before they reach governance forums. Decisions softened to protect relationships and outcomes.

None of this appears on a dashboard.

In economic terms, hidden talent functions as a form of unpaid insurance. It absorbs volatility. It smooths delivery. It reduces downside risk. And like any form of insurance, its value is only truly understood when it is gone.

There is a common leadership fallacy that productivity is evenly distributed across roles. It is not. In most organisations, a small percentage of individuals carry a disproportionate share of operational load. They do not just complete tasks. They integrate work across boundaries. They connect dots that others do not even know exist. They anticipate second- and third-order consequences. This cannot be easily replaced or redistributed.

When these individuals disengage, the loss is not linear. It is exponential.

Consider what happens when a visible performer leaves. There is disruption, indeed, but the organisation knows how to respond. Roles are advertised. Replacements are hired. Knowledge is transferred formally. When hidden talent leaves, the organisation often does not know what it has lost. Processes still exist. Documentation still exists. Job descriptions still exist. What is missing is context, timing, and judgment.

This is why leaders often say, months after a departure, something like, "We are following the process, but it no longer works the way it used to."

The process never functioned independently. Someone was making it work.

Another economic distortion occurs when hidden talent remains in place but no longer compensates for systemic weakness. Leaders then interpret the resulting friction as a need for more structure. More controls. More oversight. More layers of approval.

Each of these responses carries a cost. More meetings. Slower decisions. Increased overhead. Reduced accountability.

Ironically, these measures often further marginalise hidden talent. Those who once solved problems quietly are now required to explain themselves repeatedly, justify their decisions, and navigate bureaucratic structures that did not previously exist. The cost of working rises, while the value of contribution falls.

This is how organisations become expensive without becoming effective.

There is also a compounding effect over time that most leaders underestimate. Hidden talent acts as a stabilising force not only operationally but also culturally. They model ownership. They set informal standards. They quietly correct behaviour that does not align with the organisation's stated values. When they withdraw or leave, that informal governance disappears.

What replaces it is not chaos immediately. It is drift.

Standards soften. Exceptions multiply. People begin to push boundaries because the quiet correction is no longer there. Leaders respond with policy. Policy responds with complexity. Complexity responds with more hidden work. And the cycle accelerates.

From a financial perspective, this is deeply inefficient. You are paying more for worse outcomes.

It is also worth addressing a misconception that often arises at this point. Some leaders assume that recognising hidden talent will increase cost. That paying more attention, providing more autonomy, or adjusting reward systems will inflate budgets. In reality, the opposite is usually true.

Recognising hidden talent allows organisations to remove waste elsewhere. It reduces the need for excessive reporting. It cuts down on redundant oversight. It shortens feedback loops. It prevents rework. It lowers error rates. These efficiencies rarely show up as dramatic line items, but they compound over time.

This is why organisations that get this right often feel calmer without being complacent. There is less urgency because fewer things are breaking. Less noise because fewer people are compensating for avoidable problems. Less friction because trust has replaced control in the places where it matters most.

Another overlooked economic dimension is succession risk. Hidden talent often sits outside formal succession plans. Their roles are not considered critical because their job titles do not sound critical. When they leave, leaders scramble to understand what they did. Knowledge transfer sessions are arranged. Documents are reviewed. But what cannot be transferred quickly is a judgment built over years.

This creates a temporary competence gap that is rarely acknowledged. The organisation continues to operate, but with reduced resilience. Minor issues take longer to resolve. Decisions feel heavier. People hesitate more. Leaders sense this as increased risk, but struggle to pinpoint why.

The cost of this period is real—slower response times. Increased errors. Missed opportunities. It is rarely labelled as the cost of losing hidden talent, but that is precisely what it is.

There is also a moral hazard embedded in many reward systems. When organisations consistently reward visibility over substance, they teach people how to survive. They teach them to narrate rather than build. To escalate rather than resolve. To perform rather than protect. Over time, the talent pool adapts. People who value depth self-select out; people who value exposure self-select in.

This has long-term economic consequences. You end up with organisations that are good at talking about work, but less good at doing it. Strong in presentation, weak in execution. Agile in language, fragile in reality.

Hidden talent economics is ultimately about alignment. Alignment between what organisations say they value and what they actually reward. Alignment between the work that keeps things running and the recognition that sustains those who do it.

When this alignment exists, the return is not incremental. It is structural.

Leaders often ask how quickly they will see results if they change how they recognise and support hidden talent. The answer is that some benefits appear almost immediately, such as reduced friction. Improved decision quality. Fewer surprises. Other benefits take longer. Increased loyalty. Stronger bench strength. Cultural stability.

What matters is consistency. One-off recognition does not change the economics. Sustained attention does.

The organisations that win over time are not those that extract the most from their people, but those that protect the people who defend them. They understand that some value cannot be measured until it is missing, and they choose not to wait for absence to reveal importance.

If you take nothing else from this chapter, take this. Every organisation already pays for hidden talent. The only question is whether it pays proactively through recognition and protection, or reactively through failure, turnover, and recovery.

One approach is an investment. The other is a tax.

Leaders who understand this do not talk about hidden talent as a concept. They design around it. They look for it. They listen for it. They build systems that allow it to thrive quietly.

And in doing so, they unlock value that was always there, waiting to be seen.

SECTION III

PSYCHOLOGY AND PERCEPTION

How leaders learn to see hidden talent

The Psychology of Recognition

Why quiet achievers go unseen and how to identify them.

If you've ever watched a small boat being winched out of the sea, you'll notice something curious. Everyone stares at the vessel. The hull. The ropes. The slow sway of it rising out of the water. Very few see the quiet figure working the winch: steady hand on the crank, eyes focused on the tension in the cable, body angled just right so the movement stays smooth. If that person faltered for a moment, the whole operation would wobble. But they rarely do. Their contribution is quiet, essential, and largely overlooked.

That is what hidden talent looks like in organisations.
Not the boat. The winch operator.

They are the silent experts who hold the line, keep the structure sound, and prevent chaos from becoming catastrophe. Because they do this so naturally and reliably, leaders often assume they need nothing. They require little praise, minimal direction, and almost no maintenance.

But this assumption is that silent competence is self-sustaining. This is one of the most expensive mistakes organisations make.

Hidden talent is the quiet force that sustains an organisation. They do not ask to be noticed, they do not jostle for position, and they do not decorate their work with noise. They appear and deliver with a steadiness others rely on more than they realise. What keeps them going is rarely ego or applause. It is rarely trophies that are awarded when an organisation wants to show appreciation. Their motivation sits deeper, in a place that many leaders fail to recognise, because most workplaces are built to honour the splash, not the current. To retain these individuals, you must understand the psychological factors that motivate them and the recognition that speaks to them.

Hidden talent moves like the keel of a boat. You never see it from above the waterline, yet it's the very thing that keeps the vessel upright. The keel doesn't shimmer in the sun. It doesn't catch the wind like the sails. It doesn't draw attention like the bow cutting through the waves. But remove it, and everything that looks impressive on the surface becomes unstable. The boat will drift, spin, and eventually capsize, no matter how polished the deck looks or how brightly the flag flies. Hidden talent is the keel. Always there, never glamorous, but essential. As with the keel, their power lies in what they stabilise rather than what they display.

Intrinsic motivation is what drives this kind of person. Not because they are selfless or unusually humble, but because they are anchored by purpose. Intrinsic motivation is a strong psychological predictor of endurance, quality, and judgment. It comes from autonomy, mastery, moral standards, and the deep satisfaction of doing work well. Extrinsic motivation, the bonus, the applause, the public praise, is not meaningless, but for hidden talent, it must never replace the internal logic of why they show up in the first place. The moment a leader starts using recognition like a performance, the keel takes on water. The foundation becomes unsettled.

Most organisations misunderstand recognition because they misunderstand motivation. They design their rewards for the sails, not the keel. They create loud, performative gestures that appear impressive but address the wrong psychology. A name on a slide. A shoutout in a meeting. An award show with staged smiles. These gestures feel good to give because they are public, simple, and visible. But hidden talent does not want to become part of a show. They do not care about the photo on the intranet or the applause in a town hall. They care about being accurately understood, not theatrically acknowledged. They care about the quiet truth more than the loud gesture.

The power of subtle recognition lies in its anchoring rather than its inflation. Subtle recognition is private, specific, and sincere. It sounds like: I saw the way you handled that, and it made all the difference. It speaks to judgment, not showmanship. It respects the way they work. It meets them below the surface, where their identity lives. Research shows that this type of recognition has the strongest link to engagement because it reinforces intrinsic motivation rather than replacing it with external pressure. It stabilises the psychological keel.

Engagement itself has been misunderstood for decades. Organisations treat it like a metric, a morale score, a happiness survey. But engagement is really about identity. It concerns whether people perceive themselves in their work. Hidden talent invests identity, not display. They demonstrate ownership because their craft matters to them. But identity is fragile when unacknowledged. If the work disappears into a void, if reliability is taken for granted, if the keel is ignored long enough, the connection weakens. Not with drama. Not with complaint. But slowly, quietly, like a boat that drifts off course without anyone noticing until it's too late.

The modern workplace, driven by visibility metrics and performance theatre, often rewards the splash over the substance. Hidden talent sees this. They see promotions given to those who speak the loudest, not those who steady the ship. They see leaders mistaking noise for effectiveness. While they rarely resent it, they begin to wonder whether they belong in an environment that values appearance over integrity. Subtle recognition prevents this drift. It signals that their approach to work matters. That their stability matters. The keel is every bit as important as the sail.

Leaders often underestimate the emotional labour their hidden talent carries. They prevent crises before anyone recognises the risk. They correct mistakes quietly. They think ahead. They absorb frustration. They anchor the culture solely through their behaviour. They maintain the team's stability during storms. But even the strongest keel needs to know that someone notices the weight it carries. This is not ego. It is reciprocity. It is a basic human need to be recognised in a way that aligns with one's nature. Loud personalities need public praise. Quiet talent needs quiet truth.

The most effective leaders practise recognition as presence, not performance. They take a moment to understand the quiet patterns rather than reacting only to loud signals. They offer trust as recognition. They delegate judgment, not tasks. They grant autonomy as a sign of respect, not as a means of offloading. They affirm values, not visibility. They learn the shape of each person's keel and what it stabilises. And they never assume silence equals satisfaction.

Hidden talent responds profoundly to recognition that mirrors who they are. They do not want to shine; they want to be useful. They do not want to be celebrated; they want to be understood. They do not want to be showcased; they want their work to mean something. When a leader acknowledges the very thing the person takes pride in, not with spectacle but with sincerity, it strengthens the psychological bond more than any reward scheme ever could.

The psychology of recognition teaches us that retention is not about keeping people happy. It is about keeping people connected. Hidden talent stays where they feel seen without being dragged into the spotlight. They remain where their way of working fits the culture. They stay where their stability is valued, not exploited. They remain where the keel is recognised, quietly, as the reason the whole structure moves forward without tipping.

And they leave when they are taken for granted. They leave when surface-level performers are celebrated while deep contributors are ignored. They leave when the organisation mistakes silence for contentment. And when they leave, it is not with noise. It is with the same quiet grace with which they worked. One day, they are gone, and only then do leaders feel the hull wobble and realise what was holding the entire boat upright.

If you want to keep hidden talent, you must look beneath the surface. You must learn to recognise them in the language they speak: sincerity, precision, understanding. You must value the keel as much as the sail. Because without the keel, the brightest sail is nothing but fabric in the wind. Hidden talent does not seek attention. They are requesting to matter. And the organisations that understand this are the ones that stay upright, steady, and unstoppable, no matter the waves.

Psychology in Action

How Leaders See What Others Miss

Hidden talent is often described in organisational literature as "quiet achievers" or "silent deliverers," yet beneath these labels lies a rich tapestry of human cognition, emotion, and behaviour. Understanding these individuals requires more than observation; it requires applying psychological principles to decode how they think, what drives them, and how they navigate the pressures of organisational life. These individuals operate in a delicate balance between performance and discretion, motivation and restraint, stress and resilience. To truly understand their value, leaders must step beyond surface behaviours and explore the cognitive and emotional mechanisms that underpin their extraordinary contributions.

At the heart of hidden talent is cognitive load management. The human brain has limits. Every individual operates within a capacity to process information, solve problems, and make decisions without becoming overwhelmed. Hidden talent excels in complex, high-pressure, fluid environments, not because they are superhuman, but because they have mastered the art of managing cognitive load. They know how to prioritise, chunk tasks into manageable units, and sequence decisions in a way that preserves mental clarity. Research in cognitive psychology suggests that experts in high-performance roles engage in "schema-based processing." They develop internal mental models that allow them to recognise patterns, anticipate outcomes, and act efficiently without expending unnecessary cognitive energy. For hidden talent, these schemas are often highly refined, allowing them to navigate complexity with a calm, almost invisible confidence.

Consider Samira, a project coordinator in a technology firm. On any given day, Samira manages multiple overlapping projects, each with its own deadlines, stakeholders, and risk factors. To an outsider, her work might appear effortless. Yet behind the scenes, Samira structures her day meticulously. She uses mental frameworks to group related tasks, delegating where possible and deferring non-critical decisions to maintain clarity. She mentally tracks dependencies, anticipating potential friction before it arises. This is cognitive load management in action: by structuring her mental processes, Samira maintains high performance without visible strain, even under conditions that would overwhelm others.

Cognitive load is closely linked to stress response. The silent achievers, while calm in appearance, are often operating under significant stress. Stress, in moderation, is beneficial; it activates the body's alert systems, sharpens attention, and heightens decision-making. However, prolonged or poorly managed stress can lead to cognitive fatigue, burnout, and errors. Hidden talent demonstrates remarkable resilience to stress, not because they are unaffected by it, but because they employ strategies that modulate its impact. These strategies are psychological and behavioural. They include compartmentalisation, reframing, selective attention, and emotional regulation. In essence, they manage their stress response to maintain optimal performance.

Research in organisational psychology highlights the importance of emotional regulation in high-functioning, high-pressure roles. Hidden talent often exhibits what psychologists describe as high “emotional intelligence”, the ability to recognise one’s own emotions, understand the feelings of others, and adjust behaviour accordingly. This allows them to navigate conflict, influence peers, and maintain cohesion without relying on authority. Emotional intelligence also enables them to remain composed during crises, providing the calm anchor that allows others to perform more effectively. Emotional regulation is not suppression; it is the ability to channel energy constructively, recognising when urgency is required and when patience will yield better outcomes.

Motivation is another critical psychological factor in developing hidden talent. Traditional organisational systems often rely on extrinsic motivators, such as bonuses, promotions, recognition, and status. Hidden talent, by contrast, is typically driven by intrinsic motivation, a psychological state in which engagement is fueled by interest, mastery, and purpose rather than external reward. Self-determination theory, one of the most widely studied frameworks in motivation psychology, explains this phenomenon: humans thrive when they experience autonomy, competence, and relatedness. Hidden achievers exhibit all three. They take ownership of their work, develop mastery in their domains, and maintain strong relational connections that reinforce their sense of purpose and accountability.

Take Ethan, an operations analyst in a logistics company. Ethan rarely seeks recognition. He does not volunteer for the spotlight or lobby for promotion. Yet he consistently anticipates supply chain disruptions, proposes solutions before problems arise, and ensures delivery deadlines are met precisely. His motivation is not extrinsic; it is rooted in mastery and purpose. He derives satisfaction from solving complex problems, seeing processes run smoothly, and knowing that his work has a tangible impact. This intrinsic motivation sustains him through challenges that would demotivate others reliant on recognition and reward.

Stress, cognitive load, and motivation are intimately connected. When cognitive load exceeds capacity, tension rises, and intrinsic motivation can be undermined. Hidden talent excels by employing strategies to maintain equilibrium across these domains. They develop routines and mental habits that offload unnecessary processing, leverage relational networks to share burdens, and create personal accountability systems that reinforce purpose and clarity. These mechanisms are rarely visible yet essential to sustained performance.

Metacognition, thinking about thinking, is another defining feature of hidden talent. These individuals are acutely aware of their own cognitive processes and limitations. They reflect on how they approach problems, allocate attention, and manage energy. This self-awareness enables them to adjust strategies dynamically, anticipate bottlenecks, and maintain performance even under shifting demands. Metacognitive skill allows hidden talent to be both strategic and operational simultaneously: they see the forest and the trees, and they know which aspects require immediate intervention and which can be deferred.

A practical example is Maria, a compliance officer at a global financial institution. Maria consistently identifies regulatory risks before they escalate, yet her interventions are almost invisible to her peers. She maintains mental models of regulatory frameworks, organises her attention according to risk probability, and prioritises tasks to maximise impact while avoiding cognitive overload. When a sudden policy change is announced, Maria integrates it seamlessly into existing workflows, anticipating potential friction points and addressing them proactively. Her effectiveness is not due to effort alone; it is a product of metacognition, cognitive load management, and strategic foresight.

Another psychological principle that underpins hidden talent is resilience. While resilience is often discussed in broad terms, for these individuals it manifests in specific ways: they recover quickly from setbacks, maintain consistent performance under pressure, and adapt strategies when circumstances change. Resilience among hidden talent is enhanced by several factors: social support networks, effective stress-management techniques, and a clear sense of purpose. They often possess a growth mindset, viewing challenges as opportunities to learn rather than as threats to their competence. This mindset fuels perseverance and allows them to maintain high standards even in unpredictable environments.

Social cognition also plays a crucial role. Hidden achievers are adept at understanding others' perspectives, motivations, and behaviours. They anticipate reactions, navigate interpersonal dynamics, and influence without authority. This skill allows them to operate effectively in complex organisations, bridging gaps, resolving conflicts, and facilitating collaboration. Their influence is relational rather than positional, and it often goes unnoticed precisely because it does not seek attention. Social cognition, combined with emotional intelligence, enables hidden talent to create stability, foster trust, and facilitate outcomes in environments where formal authority alone is insufficient.

Cognitive diversity is another dimension worth exploring. Hidden talent often excels because it thinks differently from the visible leaders around them. They approach problems analytically, systemically, and creatively, drawing on insights that others may overlook. Their cognitive styles complement those of louder, more extroverted colleagues, ensuring that decisions are informed by both depth and breadth. Organisations that recognise this value benefit from balanced decision-making, increased adaptability, and more innovative solutions. Hidden talent contributes not only effort but also unique modes of thinking that enhance organisational intelligence.

Motivation in hidden talent is reinforced by purpose alignment. These individuals often align personal values with organisational goals. When work resonates with their sense of meaning, intrinsic motivation is amplified, stress is mitigated, and cognitive engagement is maximised. Leaders can support this alignment by clarifying purpose, demonstrating impact, and creating opportunities to contribute meaningfully. Importantly, alignment does not require formal authority or recognition; it requires a clear understanding of how individual contributions relate to organisational outcomes.

The intersection of cognitive load, stress management, and intrinsic motivation produces what psychologists call optimal performance zones. Hidden talent tends to operate within these zones more consistently than others. They balance challenge with capacity, maintain focus under pressure, and sustain engagement without external incentives. When conditions shift, when demands exceed capacity, or recognition systems reward the wrong behaviours, hidden talent is at risk of disengagement. Leaders who understand this dynamic can intervene to maintain equilibrium by adjusting workload, providing support, and reinforcing purpose, ensuring continued high performance.

Behavioural economics offers further insights. Hidden talent is sensitive to incentives, but it responds more strongly to autonomy, mastery, and relational influence than to monetary or status-based rewards. Traditional incentive structures can backfire, leading to disengagement when extrinsic rewards undermine intrinsic motivation. Organisations that design systems that acknowledge these psychological realities, provide autonomy, recognise expertise, and facilitate impact are more likely to retain and amplify hidden talent.

Stress responses among hidden talent are also moderated by anticipatory cognition, the ability to predict and prepare for potential disruptions. Unlike reactive performers, hidden achievers allocate cognitive resources toward foresight. They identify weak signals, anticipate bottlenecks, and intervene pre-emptively. This not only reduces the likelihood of a crisis but also preserves cognitive resources by preventing problems from escalating. Anticipatory cognition, combined with metacognition and resilience, forms a triad that enables sustained, high-level performance without visibility.

The psychology of learning is another relevant domain. A hidden talent often engages in continuous self-directed learning. They reflect on past experiences, extract lessons from them, and integrate those lessons into mental models. This iterative process enhances expertise, reduces cognitive load over time, and improves predictive accuracy in decision-making. Leaders who recognise and support learning behaviours by providing access to information, mentorship, and opportunities for experimentation reinforce the intrinsic motivation of hidden achievers and strengthen their long-term impact.

Finally, hidden talent demonstrates what can be called psychological stewardship. They act not for recognition or reward, but out of a sense of responsibility to the organisation, colleagues, and outcomes. This stewardship reflects a sophisticated integration of cognitive capacity, emotional intelligence, motivation, and ethical judgment. It explains why these individuals consistently deliver results, manage crises, and maintain organisational stability without drawing attention to themselves.

Recognising hidden talent, therefore, requires leaders to adopt a psychologically informed perspective. It is not enough to track outputs or observe behaviours superficially. Leaders must understand cognitive load, stress responses, motivation, emotional regulation, and anticipatory cognition. They must look for patterns of influence, relational intelligence, and consistent performance under pressure. By doing so, organisations can identify, nurture, and retain individuals whose contributions are critical yet often go unnoticed.

Hidden talent is psychology in action: cognitive strategies, emotional regulation, intrinsic motivation, social insight, and resilience all working seamlessly to deliver outcomes that appear effortless to those around them. Leaders who understand this psychological architecture gain a profound advantage. They can foster conditions that amplify performance, mitigate stress, and preserve motivation. They can recognise excellence that is silent but transformative. They can ensure that hidden talent not only survives but thrives, turning quiet achievement into sustained organisational success.

The challenge for every leader is clear: to see the invisible, understand the unseen, and nurture the human mechanisms that drive silent achievement. By applying psychological principles in practice, organisations unlock the potential of hidden talent. They convert unseen effort into visible outcomes, hidden expertise into systemic advantage, and silent dedication into enduring excellence.

Mapping Informal Networks

Every organisation tells two stories at the same time: the official story, neatly arranged in hierarchies, reporting lines, job titles, and governance charts; and the real story, which sits beneath the surface like the foundations of an old city, sprawling in unexpected directions. The first story is crucial because it signals accountability and authority. The second is essential because it reveals how work is actually performed. To truly lead, influence, or create change, you must learn to read the second story. That story is written in the quiet, often invisible architecture of informal networks, the relationships, conversations, trust lines, opinion gateways, hidden influencers, connectors, confidantes, sceptics, and quietly powerful individuals who shape decisions long before any official meeting takes place. Informal networks are not merely a sociable, soft side effect of working life. They are the bloodstream of the organisation. And understanding them is one of the most reliable ways to uncover influence without authority, accelerate strategy, and identify the people who genuinely drive progress behind the scenes.

It helps to think of an organisation not as a machine, with parts neatly fitted, gears turning, outputs delivered, but as an ecosystem, where every individual is a node in a living web of interactions. Some webs are dense and humming with energy; some are sparse and disconnected; some form bridges between previously distant groups; and others quietly form bottlenecks without realising it.

What matters is not only where people sit on an organisational chart, but also who they turn to, who they trust, who they share doubts with, whose opinion they quietly seek when uncertain, and whom they follow even though that person holds no formal authority. When you understand those patterns, you know power as it is actually lived.

Modern organisational research reinforces this constantly. Studies of social networks within companies consistently reveal that formal authority accounts for only part of decision-making power. Often, the individuals who are most central to the flow of information, the ones others consult for advice, clarity, or reassurance, are not managers at all but experienced, trusted colleagues. Sometimes they're quiet experts with deep institutional memory; sometimes charismatic bridge-builders who get on with everyone; sometimes fiercely competent operators who have earned credibility through years of reliability rather than hierarchy. Whatever their reason, these individuals exert outsized influence on how teams think, decide, and act. They are the quiet centre of gravity around which projects succeed or stall.

Mapping informal networks is therefore not an abstract exercise in people analytics. It's a practical art, a way of surfacing the genuine pathways of influence, trust, collaboration, and decision-making that shape the organisation's behaviour. When leaders don't understand those pathways, they unknowingly push against the system's grain. They appoint "sponsors" who have no followers. They select "change champions" who lack credibility. They design solutions that bypass the people who know how things actually work. And they're confused when resistance appears, seemingly from nowhere, not realising it travels through informal channels long before it appears in formal ones.

When leaders do understand the network beneath the structure, something interesting happens. They stop pushing change like a heavy object up a hill and start working with the system's natural flow. They involve people who matter early. They anticipate where resistance will form. They identify where decisions are really being shaped. They learn to influence without asserting authority. They discover talent that is consistently overlooked. They see where work is silently being held together by a handful of overstretched, deeply trusted individuals. And, crucially, they gain a map, not a map of positions, but a map of relationships.

The techniques for mapping informal networks have become more refined over the last decade, but the principles remain timeless. You begin by asking relational questions rather than hierarchical ones. Who do people go to for advice when something goes wrong? Who do they trust enough to share a half-formed idea? Who has the rare ability to bridge teams that rarely talk? Who do they approach when they need to bypass bureaucracy and actually get something done? These are not the sorts of questions that appear in organisational charts, but they are the questions that reveal where power lives. And when you gather them, through short surveys, interviews, digital collaboration patterns, or even ethnographic observation, you start to see a second structure emerge, a structure that is more honest and more predictive than any official one.

Translating those insights into action requires the ability to read a network not as a technologist but as a diplomat. A diagram of nodes and lines doesn't tell you the whole story. You must understand the human context: why someone is central, how they built trust, whether they are willing to support change, whether their influence is stabilising or destabilising, and whether they are overloaded or under-recognised. Influence isn't static; it shifts with events, relationships, and organisational mood. The map is merely a starting point for deeper conversations.

The real skill lies in interpreting patterns. Some networks have strong "core and periphery" structures: a tightly interconnected inner group surrounded by looser circles of contributors. When the core is healthy, ideas travel fast. When the core becomes insular, innovation dies at the boundary. Other networks feature "brokers", individuals who sit between clusters and enable communication across them. These brokers are uniquely powerful but also uniquely fragile. If they leave, become overwhelmed, or lose trust, entire communication channels collapse. Other patterns show "structural holes", gaps where two groups should connect but don't. Those gaps are often where friction, misunderstanding and duplication of effort flourish. Spotting them allows leaders to create bridges intentionally rather than by accident.

The informal network also reveals hidden bottlenecks. These are individuals who, often without malice or awareness, hold up decisions because so many roads lead to them. They might be the only person with a particular skill, the only one trusted by both sides of a conflict, or simply the only person who actually reads the details. Bottlenecks are double-edged: they show who is indispensable, but also where risk accumulates. When an organisation is dependent on a few individuals for far too much, resilience drops sharply.

One of the most valuable insights from informal networks is the identification of "connectors", people who naturally bring others together. They are the glue that holds the system together. They foster collaboration, mediate between groups, defuse tension, and accelerate decision-making. Connectors rarely have senior titles; they often operate quietly, motivated by a genuine desire to help. In nearly every major change initiative examined by organisational researchers, early involvement of connectors predicts success. Ignoring them makes the change feel forced. Include them and change spreads organically.

But the true power of mapping informal networks lies in understanding influence without authority. In a world where hierarchies are flattening and cross-functional work is the norm; leaders can no longer rely on positional power. Influence is earned through relationships, credibility, reciprocity and trust. This is where informal networks become a strategic advantage: they show you who already has the ears and hearts of the organisation. They show you who people believe, not because they must, but because they want to. They show where opinions are formed long before decisions are formalised.

Influence without authority is often misunderstood as persuasion or charm. In reality, it has more to do with understanding the network's currency. Every person has a set of currencies they value: knowledge, access, time, recognition, support, protection, and opportunity. When you understand what people value and trade fairly in those currencies, you naturally build influence. People listen to you because interacting with you helps them succeed. You become a trusted node in their network. The informal network reveals these currencies: who is known as a problem-solver, who has a gift for clarity, who has a reputation for fairness, and who is a source of stability. When you engage with these people respectfully, you build a coalition that carries momentum far beyond your formal remit.

The most effective leaders use network insight to orchestrate change, not to manipulate it. They bring connectors into early design conversations. They relieve overloaded brokers by creating formal structures around their bridging work. They identify isolated pockets of expertise and integrate them into cross-functional groups. They use the map to understand resistance not as stubbornness but as a signal from the system. They don't treat the network as a tool for surveillance or power plays, but as a living organism that needs to be nurtured.

Ethical considerations are central. Mapping informal networks reveals sensitive information: who is central, who is peripheral, who is trusted, and who is avoided. This requires transparency, consent, respect for privacy, and careful handling. The goal is never to expose individuals but to understand patterns that enable better design, collaboration, and leadership. Leaders who treat network mapping as a covert exercise inevitably damage trust. Those who treat it as a collaborative discovery build stronger cultures.

One powerful way to understand informal networks is through analogy. Imagine a large boat navigating through uncertain waters. The formal hierarchy is the helm, the captain, the first mate, and a transparent chain of command. The informal network comprises the crew below deck who know which ropes are worn, which knots hold, which planks leak, which sails catch the wind best, and which routines keep the ship steady in a storm. You can have a captain shouting orders, but if the crew below doesn't believe in the direction, the boat moves slowly, awkwardly, and at times not at all. But when the formal helm and the informal crew work in harmony, the ship slices through the water with surprising grace. Mapping informal networks is the act of stepping back from the helm, listening to the crew, understanding the ship's real workings, and then leading with that knowledge rather than ignoring it. It is understood that authority may steer the wheel, but influence pulls the ropes.

In practice, mapping informal networks begins with a few simple but powerful data-gathering questions. Instead of asking people, "Who do you report to?" you ask, "Who do you rely on?" "Whose opinion do you trust when you're uncertain?" "Who helps you when something goes wrong?" "Who would you go to if you needed to influence a difficult decision?" These questions uncover advice, trust, collaboration, and communication networks. Each one reveals a slightly different part of the informal landscape. When combined, they produce a rich, multi-layered understanding of the organisation's authentic social architecture.

Technology can support this process, but it should never replace judgment. Analytical tools can reveal communication frequency, collaboration patterns, activity clusters, and individual centrality. But numbers alone do not reveal the reasons behind influence. A highly connected person might be loved, respected, overwhelmed, or caught in the middle of dysfunction. A peripheral person might be isolated by choice or systematically excluded. The map shows the shape; only conversations reveal the meaning. Leaders who use maps without conversations risk misinterpretation. Leaders who combine both create insight.

The practical value of informal network mapping becomes evident during change initiatives. Countless examples exist of significant reforms that stalled because leadership communicated only through formal channels and ignored the system's real heartbeat. Conversely, in organisations where informal influencers were engaged early, invited to provide feedback, involved in shaping decisions, and respected as co-creators, change progressed faster and felt more authentic. People adopt what they help shape, especially when those shaping conversations do so through existing trust lines rather than top-down broadcasts.

Mapping networks also strengthens decision-making. When you understand who shapes opinion informally, you know how to socialise ideas before they reach official forums. Skilled leaders use informal networks to build understanding and alignment pre-emptively. They don't drop decisions into meetings like bricks; they float them through the network, listening, adjusting and shaping before any formality begins. This reduces resistance, increases psychological safety, and ensures decisions are more informed by the realities of the system.

A powerful but often overlooked benefit of network mapping is its ability to uncover hidden talent. Many of the most quietly influential individuals in organisations are not visible to senior leadership because they are not noisy, political, self-promoting or ambitious in traditional ways. They are the ones who get things done, who others rely on instinctively, who make teams function without fanfare. Mapping networks makes these individuals visible. It reveals the diamonds in the rough, the steady, trusted operators who carry enormous informal power. In an age where leadership pipelines suffer from visibility bias, informal network mapping offers a corrective lens that rewards substance over showmanship.

The challenges of mapping networks are not technical but cultural. Some organisations fear transparency because they worry what maps might reveal: unhealthy dependencies, silos, exclusion, over-centralisation, or under-recognition. But problems do not disappear because they remain hidden. There is a quiet bravery in choosing to look. When leaders look honestly at the informal network, they are taking the first step toward redesigning the system to work as intended. And when they do so with respect, clarity, and fairness, they create cultures in which influence is acknowledged, talent is surfaced, and collaboration becomes intentional rather than accidental.

The future of informal network mapping is evolving as AI and advanced analytics become more common, but the fundamentals remain human. AI can quickly identify patterns, reveal hidden correlations, and predict where communication bottlenecks might form. But only humans can understand emotional nuance, cultural nuance, relational trust, and the unspoken agreements that define influence. The future is not AI replacing human judgment. Still, AI amplifies it, helping leaders see what they could not otherwise notice so they can act with wisdom rather than assumption.

The most enduring lesson from mapping informal networks is simple: people follow relationships before they follow instructions. They listen to those they trust. They share truth with those who make them feel safe. They change behaviour when they believe the change is morally coherent, socially backed, and personally meaningful. The informal network is where those beliefs form. It is the quiet parliament of the organisation. And if you want to lead effectively, especially without authority, that parliament is where you must earn your voice.

To navigate an organisation well, therefore, you must learn to think in networks rather than hierarchies. Hierarchies tell you who holds the title. Networks indicate who has influence. Hierarchies tell you who signs off. Networks tell you who shapes the thinking before anything is signed. Hierarchies show positions. Networks show power. And once you understand that difference, once you can see the invisible wiring of the system, you no longer need authority to be effective. You need only connection, credibility and curiosity.

Influence without authority is not a mystical trait possessed by a gifted few. It is the natural consequence of understanding how human systems work. People will follow you if you know the network better than others, if you respect the network rather than try to dominate it, and if you contribute more value to the network than you extract. When you do this consistently, you become a node of trust. And trust is the most potent form of authority.

Mapping informal networks gives leaders a more accurate, more humane way of seeing their organisation, one that acknowledges the hidden labour, the unspoken alliances, the quiet heroes, and the subtle forces that shape behaviour. It reveals not only the organisation's structure but also its soul. When you understand the system's soul, you can lead with greater precision, empathy, and effectiveness.

Ultimately, every organisation is a boat on a vast, unpredictable sea. The formal structure may define who stands at the wheel, who charts the course, and who calls the commands. But the informal network, the relationships below deck, determines how fast that boat moves, how resilient it is in storms, and whether the crew trusts the journey enough to give their best. The wise leader maps both. The transformative leader understands that the second map, the map of influence, trust and connection, is the one that truly decides the destination.

The Work That Saves You at 3 A.M.

Every organisation has them. You might not see them at town halls, in keynote speeches, or at performance award ceremonies. They do not dominate Zoom calls, send lengthy self-promoting emails, or insist on being consulted for every decision. Yet, when deadlines loom, problems escalate, or crises strike, they are the ones who step forward. They are the silent deliverers, the quiet achievers whose value is often invisible to anyone outside the immediate sphere of their work. They are the people who ensure that organisations function, not because anyone recognises them, but because they understand, deeply, what needs to be done and do it.

The paradox of the silent deliverer is that their power lies precisely in their invisibility. Whereas organisations often celebrate visibility, loudness, and authority, the quiet achievers operate in a different currency: reliability, foresight, problem-solving, and resilience. They measure themselves by results, not applause. Their influence is practical, grounded, and persistent. And it is this influence, unheralded though it may be, that often determines whether a team succeeds or fails, a project survives or collapses, a company thrives or falters.

Consider Maya, a logistics manager in a multinational supply chain company. When a key supplier unexpectedly failed to deliver a critical shipment, the crisis room erupted in frantic discussions about alternatives, contingency plans, and blame. Maya, whose title was mid-level and whose office was tucked away at the edge of the facility, quietly pulled together a new delivery schedule, coordinated with multiple regional offices, and personally called suppliers to negotiate partial shipments. By the end of the day, the crisis had been averted. No meeting minutes mentioned her. No executive compliment arrived in her inbox. She returned to her desk and continued her work, invisible yet indispensable.

Maya's story is far from unique. Research into organisational behaviour consistently demonstrates that work is often delivered by individuals whose influence is informal, who operate outside hierarchical authority, and whose contributions are only noticed when outcomes are measured in full. A 2022 study by the Institute of Leadership & Management found that in 71% of organisations, the employees most critical to problem-solving and crisis management were not in leadership positions and were not formally recognised in succession plans. The work of these silent deliverers is foundational yet rarely celebrated or even acknowledged officially.

What distinguishes these individuals is not only competence but a particular mindset. Silent deliverers possess what organisational psychologists term "proactive responsibility", a commitment to solving problems before they escalate, coupled with an acute awareness of the impact of their actions on others. They anticipate risk, act with precision, and take ownership without being asked. Their approach to challenges is methodical and calm. They understand the intricacies of systems and processes, often better than anyone formally responsible for oversight. In short, they operate as custodians of organisational stability, guardians of continuity, and catalysts of success, all without the need for recognition or reward.

The mechanics of their work are often subtle yet profound. In moments of crisis, they act as stabilisers. While others react emotionally or focus on visible tasks, the silent deliverers map the problem, identify critical nodes, and execute solutions quietly and efficiently. They bridge gaps between teams, often operating as the connective tissue that ensures knowledge, resources, and decisions flow where they are needed. These individuals also exhibit remarkable situational awareness: they understand which levers to pull, which relationships to engage, and which processes to bend, all without disrupting broader organisational norms. Their actions are both strategic and operational, yet they rarely seek attention.

Take Liam, a systems analyst in a financial institution. During a major software rollout, unexpected glitches threatened to disrupt operations across multiple branches. While management focused on meetings, reports, and approvals, Liam remained behind the scenes, liaising with developers, testing fixes, and ensuring that customer-facing services continued uninterrupted. By the time executives became aware of the crisis, it had already been resolved. Liam's impact was massive, yet invisible. The organisation only noticed the absence of failure, not the presence of intervention. This dynamic is familiar: silent deliverers operate in spaces where success appears effortless precisely because of their preparation, foresight, and intervention.

Their invisibility is both a strength and a risk. Because their work is rarely highlighted, silent deliverers can be overlooked in promotions, performance reviews, and succession planning. They may not advocate for themselves, believing that the quality of their work should speak for itself. Organisations that fail to recognise them risk losing these individuals to burnout, disengagement, or attrition. A 2021 Gallup study found that high-performing but under-recognised employees are twice as likely to leave their organisations within three years. Silent deliverers, despite their centrality to success, are particularly vulnerable to this dynamic.

Understanding these individuals requires a shift in perception. Traditional performance assessments favour output that is visible, measurable, and attributable to an individual. Silent deliverers, by contrast, produce outcomes that are relational, emergent, and systemic. Their work is often the sum of countless micro-interventions: smoothing conflicts, realigning miscommunications, preventing errors, and maintaining continuity. Recognising their contributions requires attention to patterns rather than to single events, to networks rather than to hierarchies, and to the outcomes of work rather than to the volume of its presentation.

A practical way to identify silent deliverers is to observe informal networks. These are the webs of influence and trust that exist beneath the formal organisational chart. People instinctively turn to certain colleagues for help, guidance, or problem-solving. These individuals may not hold formal authority, yet their advice carries weight and their involvement accelerates solution development. Mapping these networks, even informally, can reveal the critical nodes that sustain organisations' effective functioning. The silent deliverers are often at the centre of these networks, providing cohesion and stability across teams, functions, and projects.

Silent deliverers are also defined by their resilience. They perform under pressure, often without support or recognition, and maintain consistency even when circumstances are adverse. They are adaptive, responding to unexpected challenges with creativity rather than panic. This resilience is not simply about enduring hardship; it is about anticipating it and preparing the organisation to withstand it. In crises, their calm, deliberate interventions prevent minor issues from escalating into systemic failures. They embody what organisational theorists describe as "operational intelligence": the ability to anticipate the practical consequences of decisions and to act in ways that minimise risk while maximising outcomes.

Consider the experience of Rachel, a project coordinator at a healthcare provider. When a sudden regulatory audit threatened to delay patient services, Rachel quietly reorganised workflows, redistributed tasks, and ensured compliance documentation was accurate and complete. No meetings were held to praise her initiative. No report was sent to leadership. Yet her actions directly prevented a cascade of delays that would have affected thousands of patients. Rachel exemplifies the essence of silent delivery: a focus on impact over visibility, and on resolution over recognition.

The work of silent deliverers is often proactive rather than reactive. They anticipate potential issues, identify bottlenecks, and take preventive measures before they arise. This anticipatory behaviour distinguishes them from those who are merely competent; it reflects organisational foresight that is rarely captured by formal metrics. In many ways, these individuals operate as the unsung architects of continuity, building invisible scaffolding that supports every function within the organisation.

Leadership plays a crucial role in harnessing the potential of silent deliverers. Organisations that recognise and nurture these individuals benefit from their reliability, judgement, and problem-solving abilities. Leaders can engage them by building trust and empowerment, providing meaningful opportunities to contribute, and creating a culture where quiet achievement is valued as much as visible performance, ensuring that silent deliverers feel acknowledged, motivated, and retained. Conversely, organisations that reward noise over impact, visibility over competence, risk alienating the very individuals who sustain their operations.

The contribution of silent deliverers is also cumulative. Their interventions, often small in isolation, accumulate over time to produce extraordinary organisational resilience. Each avoided crisis, each resolved conflict, each micro-adjustment in processes, contributes to a culture of reliability, stability, and excellence. The absence of failure, in many cases, is the most visible indicator of their presence. Organisations that ignore this dynamic mistake silence for inactivity, invisibility for irrelevance, and discretion for disengagement.

A defining feature of silent deliverers is their relational intelligence. They understand the human elements of work, trust, influence, empathy, and collaboration and use these skills to navigate complex organisational dynamics. They build relationships not for personal gain, but to ensure that work flows smoothly, decisions are informed, and conflicts are managed before they escalate. Their capacity to influence without authority often surpasses that of formal leaders who rely on positional power alone. In this sense, they are both stabilisers and accelerators: they prevent breakdowns and enable progress.

Another key insight is that silent deliverers are often intrinsically motivated. They do not seek recognition or reward. Their satisfaction comes from the work itself and the knowledge that outcomes are achieved. This intrinsic motivation aligns with self-determination theory, which posits that autonomy, mastery, and purpose drive sustained high performance. Silent deliverers exemplify this principle: they act because they care, because they know they can make a difference, and because they hold themselves accountable to standards that often exceed organisational expectations.

Yet intrinsic motivation alone is not enough to sustain silent delivery. Organisations must create structures that support these individuals, even if indirectly. Recognition need not be public or performative; it can be as simple as ensuring their expertise is consulted, their workload is manageable, and their contributions are documented for future reference. Mentorship, access to resources, and opportunities for skill development can reinforce their impact without imposing unwanted visibility. Organisations that do this not only retain their silent deliverers but amplify their influence across the system.

Technology can support silent delivery, but it cannot replace it. Digital tools, workflow systems, and analytics can streamline processes, alert leaders to risks, and automate routine tasks. However, the judgment, foresight, and relational skill that silent deliverers provide remain uniquely human. Technology may enhance visibility of outcomes, but it cannot replicate the nuanced, anticipatory, and contextually aware interventions that define silent achievement. The human element, observation, intuition, problem-solving, and discretion remains irreplaceable.

Silent deliverers also play a pivotal role in organisational learning. By observing patterns, resolving recurring problems, and creating informal knowledge repositories, they transmit institutional memory that ensures continuity despite turnover, restructuring, or crisis. Their work preserves lessons learned and embeds them into everyday practices, often without formal documentation. In this sense, they are custodians of knowledge, ensuring that the organisation does not repeat mistakes and can build on past successes.

The cumulative effect of these contributions is profound. Organisations with a strong base of silent deliverers tend to be more resilient, adaptive, and reliable. They navigate crises with less disruption, execute complex projects more consistently, and maintain higher levels of operational stability. Yet, without deliberate recognition and engagement, these advantages remain invisible, their actual value obscured by the organisation's focus on visible outputs and performative leadership.

Identifying silent deliverers requires deliberate observation, active listening, and a willingness to look beyond formal structures. It involves asking questions differently: who do people rely on when things go wrong? Whose advice is trusted implicitly? Who resolves issues before they escalate? Who maintains cohesion across teams without formal authority? These questions reveal patterns of influence, reliability, and skill that formal charts and reports cannot capture. Once identified, these individuals can be supported, leveraged, and celebrated in ways that align with their intrinsic motivation rather than forcing performative behaviour.

The silent deliverers are not anomalies or exceptions. They are a recurring and critical feature of every successful organisation.

Their presence explains why some teams succeed against the odds, why some projects deliver despite turbulence, and why specific organisations maintain continuity in the face of change. They are the quiet backbone, the stabilising agents, and the unsung heroes whose work enables others to shine.

Ultimately, the lesson of the silent deliverers is both profound and straightforward: the most valuable contributions are often invisible. Leadership must learn to see what cannot be measured by volume, reports, or applause. Organisations must cultivate cultures that respect discretion, reward reliability, and recognise impact beyond visibility. Only then can the silent deliverers thrive, and only then can organisations achieve the full potential of the talent they already possess.

The challenge, therefore, is to cultivate attention without intrusion, recognition without forcing performance, and influence without authority. Silent deliverers remind us that the loudest voices are not always the most important, that resilience is often quiet, and that impact usually goes unseen. By learning to identify, support, and value these individuals, organisations gain more than efficiency or productivity; they gain stability, innovation, and an enduring capacity to deliver under any circumstance.

And so, to every leader, manager, or team member reading this: look closer. Observe who quietly resolves the problems no one else notices. Notice who bridges the gaps between teams, who anticipates crises before they arrive, and who keeps the organisation functioning when all else seems chaotic. These are the silent deliverers. They do not ask for recognition, but they deserve it. They do not seek reward, but they earn it. They do not demand attention, but they command respect. And when an organisation finally acknowledges them, it is not only stronger, but also transformed.

SECTION IV

ACTIVATING HIDDEN TALENT

Turning insight into action

Finding and Nurturing Hidden Talent

There is another layer to recognising hidden talent that only becomes visible over time: the discipline of restraint. Many leaders believe that once they have identified capability, the next step is to act quickly. They want to formalise it, promote it, showcase it, or replicate it. With visible performers, this instinct often works. With hidden talent, it can do real harm.

Hidden talent often thrives because it is allowed to operate below the noise line. The moment it is pulled into constant explanation, justification, or performance, its effectiveness diminishes. Leaders must therefore learn not only how to identify these individuals but also how to resist the urge to overmanage them once identified. Recognition, in this context, is not extraction. It is protection.

This requires leaders to develop a different sense of value. Instead of asking how to get more out of someone, the better question becomes how to remove obstacles so their contribution can continue uninterrupted. Often this means shielding them from unnecessary meetings, insulating them from politics, and intervening when others attempt to appropriate their work without understanding it.

One of the most reliable indicators of hidden talent is how people respond when complexity increases. In moments of ambiguity, most people seek clarity from authority. Hidden talent seeks clarity from the problem itself. They return to first principles. They trace dependencies. They test assumptions quietly before forming conclusions. Leaders who pay attention will notice that these individuals often ask fewer questions, but better ones.

Another signal lies in how individuals react to recognition itself. Visible performers tend to lean into it. They expand their presence. They amplify their narrative. Hidden talent often does the opposite. They deflect attention. They redirect credit. They appear uncomfortable with praise that feels imprecise or inflated. This is not insecurity. It is integrity.

Leaders who misinterpret this response often conclude that these individuals lack ambition. In reality, their ambition is oriented differently. They want the system to work. They want the outcome to hold. They want the organisation to succeed without unnecessary drama. Their satisfaction comes from things functioning as they should.

Understanding this orientation is critical when considering development pathways. Traditional career models reward upward movement, increased visibility, and broader spans of control. Hidden talent does not always aspire to this trajectory. Forcing it can result in disengagement or burnout. Development, for these individuals, is more often about deepening expertise, expanding influence laterally, or increasing autonomy rather than increasing exposure.

This is where many organisations lose hidden talent despite good intentions. They offer promotion as the only form of recognition. They assume advancement must look the same for everyone. When hidden talent hesitates or declines, leaders interpret this as a lack of drive and shift their attention elsewhere. In doing so, they miss an opportunity to design more flexible, more human models of contribution.

Another overlooked aspect of finding hidden talent is the role of middle management. Frontline managers often have the clearest view of who is actually doing the work. They see who steps in when things wobble. They know who others trust. But they are rarely asked this explicitly. Leadership discussions tend to focus upward rather than downward. Who presents well. Who leads meetings confidently. Who appears ready.

Leaders who want to surface hidden talent must learn to ask different questions of their managers. Not who is high potential, but who would worry you most if they left quietly. Not who speaks up most, but who others rely on without realising it. These questions shift the lens from aspiration to dependency.

Dependency is uncomfortable to confront. It exposes fragility. But it is also where the most valuable insight lives.

There is also an emotional discipline required in nurturing hidden talent. These individuals often take on responsibility without formal authority, which can create tension with peers. Others may feel threatened or overshadowed, even if nothing overt is happening. Leaders must be alert to this dynamic. Protecting hidden talent sometimes means managing the environment around them, not the individual themselves.

This can involve setting clear boundaries regarding ownership, intervening when credit is misallocated, or making expectations explicit to prevent quiet contributors from being overloaded. It also means being prepared to have difficult conversations with those who benefit from visibility but contribute less substance.

Leaders often avoid these conversations because they are uncomfortable. But avoidance has a cost. When hidden talent consistently carries more than its share of the load, resentment can build quietly. Because these individuals rarely complain, the resentment is not expressed directly. It manifests as withdrawal, fatigue, or indifference. By the time it is noticed, repair is complex.

Nurturing hidden talent, therefore, requires vigilance. Not surveillance, but attentiveness. Leaders must check in without interrogating. They must listen without extracting. They must signal value without turning it into performance.

One practical way to do this is through the review process for work. Many organisations focus on outputs rather than processes. What was delivered? Was it on time? Did it meet expectations? While important, this often obscures the most valuable contributions. Leaders should also ask how the work was delivered and where friction was absorbed. What almost went wrong. Who intervened quietly.

These questions surface invisible work. They also communicate to the organisation that such work matters.

Another effective practice is to rotate leaders through shadowing roles. Sitting alongside operational teams and observing without directing. This is not about oversight. It is about exposure. Leaders who do this regularly develop a more accurate picture of where competence lives. They also develop humility, which is essential for recognising talent that does not appear to be leadership.

Technology can support this, but it cannot replace it. Data can highlight patterns, but it cannot explain them. Leaders must be sufficiently present to interpret what they observe. Hidden talent is often contextual. Its value emerges in how it responds to specific pressures, not in abstract metrics.

Retention, at this level, becomes an ethical issue as much as a strategic one. When organisations benefit disproportionately from individuals who are rarely acknowledged, there is an implicit imbalance. Leaders who recognise this must decide whether they are willing to address it. Doing so may require rethinking reward structures, redefining success, and challenging entrenched norms.

This is not easy work. It requires leaders to give up some comfort. It asks them to value contributions that cannot always be showcased. It demands patience in a culture that often rewards immediacy.

But the return is profound.

Organisations that genuinely nurture hidden talent develop a depth that is difficult to replicate. They are less dependent on heroics. Less vulnerable to sudden loss. More capable of absorbing shock. Their performance is steadier, their culture quieter, their outcomes more reliable.

Leaders in such organisations often find that their role changes. They spend less time resolving crises and more time shaping direction. They trust their teams more because that trust is earned through consistent, quiet competence. They are surprised less often because fewer things escalate unexpectedly.

This is not because people work harder. It is because work is distributed more intelligently.

The act of finding and nurturing hidden talent is therefore not a separate leadership skill. It is foundational. It shapes how leaders listen, decide, reward, and intervene. It changes the questions they ask and the signals they respond to.

Ultimately, this practice reflects a more profound philosophy. That leadership is not about being the most visible person in the room, but about creating conditions where the most capable people can do their best work without obstruction. That success is not always loud. That value is not always obvious. The most important work often happens when no one is watching.

Leaders who embrace this philosophy do not simply uncover hidden talent. They build organisations that deserve it.

And in doing so, they ensure that quiet competence is not an accident, but a defining feature of how work gets done.

Why You Are Not Hiring Hidden Talent

Most organisations believe they have a talent problem. What they actually have is a selection problem.

Hidden talent is not rare in the market. It is rare in shortlists.

This is not because these individuals are hard to find. This is because most hiring processes are designed to filter them out before they reach a decision-maker. The irony is uncomfortable. The very systems that leaders trust to identify capability are often optimised to reward confidence, fluency, and performance under artificial conditions rather than judgment, depth, and reliability under real-world conditions.

I have sat on hundreds of interview panels across regions and functions. The pattern is remarkably consistent. Candidates are assessed on how well they present themselves, not how well they think. On how clearly, they speak, not how accurately they reason. On how confidently they answer, not how carefully they decide.

Hidden talent struggles here, not because they lack competence, but because they refuse to simplify complexity for effect.

Interviews reward speed. Hidden talent values precision.
Interviews reward certainty. Hidden talent respects nuance.
Interviews reward articulation. Hidden talent prioritises accuracy.

When asked a question, the visible performer answers immediately. The hidden performer pauses. They ask for clarification. They think. In an interview setting, that pause is often misread as hesitation or lack of confidence. In real work, it is a sign of responsibility.

This bias is reinforced by how hiring decisions are made. Panels discuss who impressed, who came across well, and who seemed to have leadership potential. These are subjective impressions dressed up as judgment. They favour those who perform well in the room, not those who perform well over time.

Hidden talent does not perform for rooms. They perform for outcomes.

There is another structural problem. Job descriptions themselves often signal who is welcome and who is not. They are filled with language about influence, visibility, pace, and presence. They reward those who seek visibility rather than those who seek to build.

When hidden talent reads these descriptions, they often self-select out. They assume the organisation values a style that it does not embody. They presume their strengths will not be recognised. And they are usually right.

Even when hidden talent makes it through the initial stages, reference checking introduces another distortion. References are often asked to comment on leadership presence, communication style, and visibility. The quiet achiever receives praise that sounds faint by comparison. Reliable. Solid. Dependable. Trusted.

These words should halt the hiring process. Instead, they are often treated as faint praise.

This is how organisations systematically hire noise.

The consequences are subtle at first. Teams are staffed with articulate individuals who can explain their work well but struggle to perform the most complex aspects of it. Decision-making becomes faster but less grounded. Problems are escalated more often because fewer people feel responsible for quietly resolving them.

Leaders then respond by adding more oversight, more meetings, more reporting. They attempt to manage around the capability gap they unknowingly created.

There is a better way, but it requires leaders to unlearn some habits.

If you want to hire hidden talent, you must change what you look for and how you look.

Start with how you interview.

Ask candidates to walk you through how they approached a complex problem, not what the outcome was. Listen for how they frame risk, how they consider trade-offs, and how they address uncertainty. Do not interrupt silence. Let them think. Please note whether they ask clarifying questions before answering. That behaviour predicts judgment far better than fluency.

Introduce work-based assessment that mirrors reality. Not presentations designed to impress, but scenarios designed to reveal thinking. Give candidates time. Allow iteration. See how they respond when they realise the problem is more complex than it first appeared.

Pay attention to how candidates talk about credit. Hidden talent often deflects praise and speaks in terms of team outcomes rather than personal wins. This is not a lack of ambition. It is a different orientation to success.

Change how you evaluate communication. Being concise is not the same as being shallow. Being careful is not the same as being unsure. Leaders must learn to distinguish between confidence and competence. They are not the same thing.

Finally, examine who makes hiring decisions. If your interview panels are dominated by the same visible performers, you already reward internally, you will replicate the same bias at the point of entry. Diversity of thought requires diversity of evaluators.

Hidden talent recognises hidden talent.

The goal is not to eliminate visible performers. Organisations need both. The goal is balance. A system that only hires one type of contributor becomes fragile. It looks impressive until it is tested.

If you want organisations that can absorb complexity, withstand pressure, and operate without constant escalation, you must hire people who do not require constant oversight to be effective.

That starts with recognising that your current hiring process may be selecting against the very people you most need.

Hidden talent does not fail interviews because of a lack of ability. They fail interviews because the interview was never designed to see them.

If you want different outcomes, you must be willing to make other choices.

Empowering Without Spotlight

Every leader understands the temptation of the spotlight. Meetings, presentations, awards, and performance dashboards all celebrate visibility. Organisations instinctively reward the loudest, the most assertive, the most visible contributors. And yet, as we have seen in earlier chapters, the people who often drive the most meaningful outcomes are precisely those who avoid attention. They do not volunteer for recognition. They do not dominate discussions. They do not position themselves as the heroes. These individuals, the hidden talent, require a different form of leadership: one that empowers without forcing visibility, recognises without creating pressure, and nurtures responsibility without triggering burnout.

The first principle of empowering without spotlight is trust. Trust is not granted automatically; it must be earned and consistently reinforced. Hidden talent thrives when leaders demonstrate confidence in their ability to manage complex tasks and make decisions. This is not a laissez-faire approach that abandons oversight; it is a structured confidence that allows autonomy within boundaries. Leaders who micromanage, demand constant reporting, or impose rigid processes inadvertently undermine the very qualities that make these individuals valuable. Empowerment begins with the simple, yet profound act of signalling, "I trust you to deliver, and I am here to support, not to oversee unnecessarily."

Consider Sophie, a senior operations specialist at a multinational manufacturing firm. Sophie consistently anticipates production bottlenecks, solves logistical challenges, and manages cross-team dependencies, all without seeking recognition. Her manager recognised this quietly, offering her expanded responsibility in scheduling and process oversight, but without adding public reporting requirements or formal visibility. Sophie's performance soared, and her sense of ownership deepened, precisely because her manager provided influence without a spotlight She felt trusted, valued, and engaged, yet not pressured by performative expectations. This subtle approach exemplifies the psychological principle that autonomy fuels intrinsic motivation, particularly for hidden talent.

Autonomy is indeed central. Self-determination theory, widely applied in organisational psychology, identifies autonomy as a key driver of intrinsic motivation. When hidden talent is given latitude to make decisions, experiment with processes, and apply expertise without constant oversight, engagement and performance increase. Conversely, forcing visibility through mandatory presentations, frequent status updates, or performative recognition can be demotivating. For quiet achievers, recognition that demands public performance often conflicts with their natural working style, creating stress rather than motivation. Empowerment without spotlight respects this distinction.

The second principle is responsibility aligned with capability. Hidden talent is not only competent; they often demonstrate a nuanced understanding of risk, process, and relational dynamics. Leaders can leverage this by providing opportunities to exercise judgment, influence outcomes, and manage complexity.

Importantly, this responsibility must be structured to avoid overwhelming cognitive load. Assigning too many high-stakes tasks without sufficient support, or coupling responsibility with performative visibility, risks burnout. The art of empowerment lies in balancing challenge with capacity, providing meaningful influence while preserving cognitive and emotional energy.

Take Arun, a mid-level project manager in a global software firm. Arun was entrusted with coordinating multiple development teams across different time zones. Rather than spotlighting his role to executives, his manager focused on clarifying objectives, ensuring access to resources, and providing support when needed. Arun thrived. He managed dependencies, mitigated risk, and consistently delivered outcomes. He felt empowered because responsibility was aligned with capability, and his autonomy was preserved. He was not performing for an audience; he was performing because the work itself mattered, and his influence was meaningful.

Recognition without pressure is the third principle. Hidden talent often does not seek recognition, yet recognition remains critical to engagement. Leaders can provide recognition in ways that reinforce contribution without creating a performative burden. This can include private messages, team-level acknowledgement, or targeted opportunities to contribute strategically without public exposure. The key is to make recognition meaningful but unobtrusive, reinforcing value without altering the individual's preferred working style.

Research in organisational behaviour shows that recognition has multiple dimensions: visibility, specificity, and relevance. For hidden talent, the most effective recognition is specific and relevant but not necessarily visible. It reinforces the connection between effort and outcome, supports intrinsic motivation, and signals appreciation without demanding public performance. Leaders who master this approach ensure that hidden achievers feel valued while remaining comfortable in their low-profile working style.

Another critical element is influence without authority. Hidden talent often operates effectively in the absence of formal authority. Leaders can amplify their impact by providing platforms on which their expertise is leveraged without imposing hierarchical visibility. This may involve enabling them to participate in cross-functional problem-solving, granting them access to critical decision-making processes, or facilitating informal networks in which their knowledge is valued. Influence in this context is subtle, relational, and systemic. It allows hidden talent to shape outcomes while preserving their natural discretion.

Consider the case of Lila, a compliance analyst in a financial institution. Lila had no formal authority over operational teams, yet she consistently identified potential regulatory risks before they became critical. Her manager empowered her by incorporating her insights into planning sessions and ensuring that her recommendations were implemented, without requiring her to present them publicly. Lila's influence grew organically, her motivation remained intrinsic, and the organisation avoided unnecessary visibility pressure that could have undermined her effectiveness.

Psychological safety is a fourth principle. Hidden talent operates best in environments where errors are treated as learning opportunities, questions are welcomed, and contributions are respected regardless of visibility. Leaders must foster environments where individuals feel safe to take initiative, experiment, and innovate without fear of public scrutiny or judgment. Psychological safety reduces stress, mitigates the risk of cognitive overload, and encourages proactive problem-solving, all critical factors for sustaining hidden talent.

Empowering without a spotlight also requires attention to workload and cognitive capacity. Hidden achievers are often high performers precisely because they manage tasks efficiently, anticipate challenges, and streamline processes. However, overloading them with additional responsibilities or coupling critical tasks with visibility demands can lead to cognitive fatigue and burnout. Leaders must monitor both objective workload and perceived cognitive demand, ensuring that empowerment enhances performance without undermining wellbeing.

A subtle but powerful technique is delegated decision-making with support. Rather than micromanaging or requiring frequent status updates, leaders can delegate authority for specific domains, while providing a safety net of guidance and resources. This approach enhances autonomy, builds confidence, and preserves intrinsic motivation. Hidden talent thrives when empowered to make meaningful decisions, knowing that support is available if needed, but not imposed unnecessarily.

Communication style is equally important. Leaders must adapt messaging to respect discretion. Directives should be clear, objectives explicit, and expectations manageable. Feedback should be precise, constructive, and aligned with outcomes rather than performative visibility. Public recognition should be optional, allowing hidden achievers to choose how, when, and if they are acknowledged. Effective communication in this context balances transparency with respect for individual working styles.

Mentorship and development can also be structured to support empowerment without spotlight. Traditional mentorship often assumes visibility, promotion, or public exposure as goals. For hidden talent, mentorship should focus on strategic influence, skill development, and network building. Mentors can provide guidance on complex problem-solving, navigating organisational dynamics, and expanding impact without forcing performative behaviour. This form of mentorship strengthens both competence and confidence, ensuring that empowerment is sustainable.

Leaders must also consider network facilitation. Hidden talent often operates effectively through informal networks rather than formal hierarchies. Empowerment can involve connecting these individuals with key colleagues, providing access to knowledge flows, and enabling their influence to propagate without imposing visibility demands. By enhancing the relational infrastructure, leaders amplify impact while respecting discretion.

Feedback loops are another mechanism for empowering without a spotlight. Regular, focused feedback reinforces effectiveness and alignment without requiring public exposure. Feedback should highlight outcomes, problem-solving, and relational influence. It should emphasise impact rather than effort or visibility. When feedback is delivered in a psychologically safe, private, and constructive manner, it strengthens motivation and supports sustainable empowerment.

Recognition rituals can be reimagined. Instead of public awards or grand gestures, organisations can create subtler forms of acknowledgement: private notes, team acknowledgements, or strategic inclusion in decision-making. These rituals convey appreciation, reinforce intrinsic motivation, and sustain engagement without creating performance pressure. Over time, these practices cultivate a culture where quiet achievement is respected, valued, and amplified.

Empowerment without spotlight also involves strategic visibility for influence, not for recognition. Hidden talent should be positioned to maximise organisational impact without forcing them into uncomfortable public roles. This might include providing input in strategy meetings, participating in cross-functional initiatives, or leading internal problem-solving discussions. The key is influence without performative exposure: their contributions shape outcomes without requiring them to act in ways that compromise their working style.

Stress management remains central. Hidden talent often carries significant responsibility without visibility, which can lead to hidden stress. Leaders must actively monitor stress indicators, provide support, and encourage resilience-building strategies, including task prioritisation, pacing, and autonomy over scheduling. Empowerment is sustainable only when cognitive and emotional load are managed, and when hidden achievers feel supported rather than isolated.

A final principle is alignment with purpose. Hidden talent thrives when their work is meaningful and aligned with both personal values and organisational goals. Leaders can enhance empowerment by clarifying how tasks contribute to outcomes, illustrating the broader impact, and connecting responsibility to organisational purpose. When purpose is clear, autonomy is preserved, and recognition is subtle, engagement and performance flourish naturally.

Empowering without a spotlight is not passive; it is active, deliberate, and nuanced. It requires understanding individual working styles, anticipating stressors, providing support without oversight, and reinforcing impact without forcing visibility. Leaders who master this approach unlock extraordinary potential, creating environments where hidden talent can thrive sustainably, deliver consistently, and influence outcomes profoundly.

Consider Noor, a data analyst at a healthcare provider. She consistently identifies inefficiencies in patient scheduling, but she avoids meetings and prefers to work quietly. Her manager empowered her by providing access to the scheduling team, granting authority to implement changes, and privately acknowledging outcomes. Noor's influence expanded significantly, patient flow improved, and she remained fully engaged, precisely because empowerment respected discretion.

Empowering without a spotlight transforms not only individuals but also organisations. It strengthens resilience, increases adaptability, and enhances capacity for sustained delivery. Hidden talent becomes more confident, more innovative, and more invested, while leaders gain reliable performance, foresight, and relational stability. The organisation benefits from a foundation of quiet, consistent achievement that complements visible leadership without conflict.

Ultimately, the lesson is clear: leadership is not about shining the light on everyone, nor is it about constant supervision or performative recognition. Leadership in the context of hidden talent is about enabling influence, amplifying capability, and nurturing responsibility in ways that preserve autonomy, protect well-being, and respect working style. It is about creating conditions in which contributions flourish silently, outcomes improve visibly, and hidden achievers thrive without burnout or exposure.

Empowering without spotlight requires a combination of trust, autonomy, aligned responsibility, subtle recognition, network facilitation, psychological safety, strategic visibility, stress management, and purpose alignment. Leaders who integrate these principles create environments where hidden talent is engaged, motivated, and maximally effective. They turn quiet capability into systemic advantage, invisible effort into sustained outcomes, and reserved dedication into organisational transformation.

For every leader committed to recognising, nurturing, and leveraging hidden talent, the task is both simple and profound: create space, provide influence, offer support, and trust that excellence will emerge, quietly but powerfully. By doing so, organisations unlock the full potential of their most valuable resource, the individuals who deliver results without applause, who influence without authority, and who sustain success without recognition. Empowerment without a spotlight is not only possible but also essential for organisational resilience, performance, and enduring success.

Creating Talent Maps

Visualising Hidden Value in Your Organisation

Organisations that excel in recognising hidden talent understand that informal recognition alone is insufficient. Knowing who delivers quietly, who solves problems behind the scenes, and who consistently prevents crises is vital, but translating this knowledge into strategic action requires documentation, mapping, and intentional alignment. Creating talent maps is the process by which organisations systematically record skills, capabilities, and potential, transforming the invisible contributions of hidden achievers into actionable organisational intelligence. This is not merely a bureaucratic exercise; it is a strategic practice that enables decision-making, optimises talent deployment, and deliberately and sustainably aligns individual strengths with business priorities.

At its core, a talent map functions as a living reflection of organisational capability. It captures not only the skills that individuals formally possess but also their tacit knowledge, problem-solving agility, relational influence, and capacity for adaptation. Hidden talent, by definition, often operates outside the formal spotlight, making its abilities less visible through conventional performance metrics. A talent map reveals these capabilities, turning anecdotal insight into structured understanding. Leaders gain a multidimensional view of who can be relied upon, who can step into critical roles, and who can drive strategic initiatives without formal authority.

The first step in creating a talent map is to observe and collect data. Observation requires deliberate attention to patterns of behaviour, collaboration, and influence. Which employees consistently intervene before a problem escalates? Whose advice is sought by peers across teams? Who navigates organisational complexity with calm, effective precision? These questions reveal informal influence and operational mastery yet must be systematically captured. Data can be gathered through multiple channels: project outcomes, peer feedback, manager assessments, cross-functional collaboration records, and even subtle behavioural indicators such as initiative-taking, problem anticipation, and relational support.

Technology can support this process, but it cannot replace human judgment. Analytical tools can track task completion, collaboration networks, and performance outcomes, providing quantitative insight into potential hidden talent. However, the qualitative nuances, foresight, creativity, relational intelligence, resilience, require careful human interpretation. Observation, combined with structured data collection, provides the most reliable foundation for talent mapping.

Once information is gathered, it must be categorised and structured. A comprehensive talent map considers multiple dimensions: skills, capabilities, potential, motivation, and influence. Skills capture technical proficiency and domain knowledge; capabilities reflect problem-solving agility, adaptability, and decision-making quality; potential encompasses growth capacity, leadership aptitude, and the ability to assume more complex roles; motivation identifies intrinsic and extrinsic drivers; and influence assesses relational impact, collaboration, and informal leadership. Capturing these dimensions allows organisations to understand both what individuals can do and how they can contribute strategically.

Consider a hypothetical example. In a financial services firm, a project team member, Daniel, consistently anticipates regulatory compliance challenges and proposes solutions before issues arise. Daniel has strong analytical skills, demonstrates foresight and initiative, could lead cross-functional projects in the future, is intrinsically motivated by problem-solving, and holds relational influence with peers despite lacking formal authority. Documenting each of these dimensions in a talent map creates a holistic view of his contribution and potential, enabling strategic deployment and development planning.

The next step is alignment with organisational priorities. A talent map is not valuable if it exists in isolation; its purpose is to connect individual capabilities with business objectives. This requires an understanding of current and future organisational needs. What skills will be critical to achieving strategic goals? Which roles require rapid problem-solving, cross-functional coordination, or crisis management? Where might the organisation experience capability gaps in the coming years? By overlaying individual talent data with organisational priorities, leaders can make informed decisions about deployment, succession planning, and development initiatives.

One practical approach is the use of heatmapping. In this method, employees are assessed against critical dimensions, such as expertise in key functions, problem-solving effectiveness, and influence within informal networks. Individuals with high capability and low visibility can then be identified as hidden talent with significant strategic value. This visual representation allows leaders to quickly see where strengths reside, where gaps exist, and where development resources should be focused. Heatmaps also facilitate scenario planning: what would happen if a high-performing individual departed? Which hidden achievers can step in without disruption? The clarity provided by visual talent maps transforms planning from reactive to proactive.

Creating talent maps also supports succession planning. Hidden talent often possesses the skills and relational influence necessary to assume more visible or complex roles, but their potential may remain untapped if unrecognised. Talent maps enable organisations to anticipate future needs and prepare individuals for higher responsibility without forcing immediate visibility or performative exposure. This mitigates risk, preserves organisational stability, and ensures critical functions continue to operate seamlessly during change.

Documenting capabilities in context is essential. Hidden talent does not operate in a vacuum. Team dynamics, relational networks, and specific organisational conditions often amplify their effectiveness. Talent maps should capture not only individual skills but also how those skills interact with colleagues, stakeholders, and processes. For instance, an individual may excel at problem-solving when collaborating with specific teams but be less effective in a different context. Mapping these nuances ensures accurate assessment and strategic alignment, enabling leaders to deploy talent where it will have the most significant impact.

Development pathways are another critical component of talent mapping. Once capabilities and potential are documented, leaders can design personalised growth plans that respect working style, cognitive load, and intrinsic motivation. Hidden talent often thrives in roles that maintain autonomy, challenge, and alignment with purpose. Development plans can include lateral moves that broaden influence, mentorship that enhances strategic impact, or project assignments that leverage strengths while expanding capabilities. A well-constructed talent map links observation, assessment, and development into a coherent framework for continuous growth.

Engaging employees in the talent mapping process also has benefits. When individuals see that their contributions are recognised and strategically aligned, engagement and motivation increase. This is particularly true for hidden talent, who may not seek recognition publicly but respond positively to signals that their work is valued and trusted. By involving employees in assessment and planning conversations, while respecting their discretion and autonomy, organisations reinforce alignment, commitment, and readiness to contribute.

An often-overlooked element is the capture of tacit knowledge. Hidden talent frequently holds critical institutional knowledge, process insights, and problem-solving heuristics that are not codified in formal documentation. Talent maps can include qualitative notes on expertise, workflow efficiencies, and relational influence. Documenting this tacit knowledge ensures organisational continuity, preserves intellectual capital, and enables leaders to leverage insights for strategic advantage.

Organisations that excel in talent mapping also integrate informal network analysis. As discussed in previous chapters, influence without authority is a hallmark of hidden talent. Talent maps should include relational indicators: who do colleagues turn to for guidance? Whose advice is sought across teams? Who consistently facilitates outcomes behind the scenes? Capturing these networks within the talent map creates a dual view of organisational capability, combining formal skills with informal influence, which enables more precise strategic deployment and risk management.

Regular review and updating are critical. Talent maps are living documents, not static records. Skills, capabilities, and potential evolve; organisational priorities shift; and hidden talent may take on new responsibilities or acquire new expertise. Frequent review cycles, informed by observation, feedback, and performance outcomes, ensure that the talent map remains accurate, actionable, and relevant. Organisations that neglect this dynamic aspect risk relying on outdated data, thereby undermining strategic alignment and limiting the effectiveness of deployment decisions.

Integration with business strategy is the ultimate goal. Talent maps should not be siloed within human resources or leadership teams; they must inform operational planning, succession, innovation initiatives, and risk mitigation. For example, when planning a new product launch, leaders can consult the talent map to identify individuals whose capabilities and relational influence are critical to success. When anticipating leadership transitions, the map reveals who can step in seamlessly without disruption. When addressing complex challenges, hidden talent with the right combination of skills and informal authority can be strategically deployed for maximum impact.

Another advantage of talent mapping is its contribution to risk management. Hidden talent often stabilises critical processes and prevents issues from escalating. If these individuals leave or are underutilised, organisations face hidden vulnerabilities. Mapping capabilities and influence enable leaders to identify potential single points of failure and to ensure redundancy, thereby mitigating operational risks associated with reliance on invisible contributors.

Implementation requires careful cultural alignment. Hidden talent thrives in environments that respect autonomy, recognise contributions without forcing visibility, and value substance over spectacle. Talent mapping initiatives should therefore be framed as tools for empowerment and development, rather than as surveillance or ranking exercises. Transparency, privacy, and respect for working style are essential; otherwise, the very individuals the organisation seeks to develop may disengage.

Finally, talent maps create a strategic language for hidden talent. They provide a framework for communicating individual capability, potential, and influence in ways that senior leadership, operational managers, and human resources can understand and act on. They turn informal knowledge into structured insight, anecdotal observations into organisational intelligence, and invisible contributions into actionable strategy. The creation of a talent map signals organisational sophistication: a recognition that success depends on both visible and hidden contributors, and that both must be deliberately understood and aligned with strategic priorities.

Consider a multinational consulting firm that implemented a comprehensive talent mapping initiative. They documented the skills, relational influence, and problem-solving agility of hidden contributors across regional offices. When a sudden regulatory challenge emerged in a critical market, the firm could strategically deploy hidden talent: individuals who were not visible in leadership meetings, but who possessed the knowledge, networks, and decision-making capacity to resolve the crisis. The result was seamless problem resolution, minimal disruption, and a reinforcement of the organisation's competitive advantage.

In conclusion, creating talent maps is both an art and a science. It involves observation, data collection, qualitative and quantitative assessment, relational analysis, alignment with organisational priorities, and continuous updating. Talent maps provide leaders with the tools to identify hidden talent, understand capability in context, and deploy individuals strategically to maximise impact. They transform informal recognition into actionable intelligence, tacit knowledge into documented capability, and invisible contribution into strategic advantage.

Hidden talent exists in every organisation, and the challenge is to make their capabilities visible without forcing performance for recognition. Talent mapping bridges this gap. It respects autonomy, amplifies influence, preserves motivation, and aligns individual capability with business priorities. By investing in this practice, organisations gain clarity, agility, and foresight. They ensure that the silent achievers, the problem-solvers, the stabilisers, the quiet innovators are recognised, understood, and positioned to deliver impact where it matters most. Talent maps do not merely record who does what; they reveal who matters, why they matter, and how they can be strategically leveraged to achieve organisational success.

Amplifying Impact

Organisations often measure impact by visibility: who speaks the loudest in meetings, whose work is showcased, and who carries a title that signals authority. Yet the most profound effect frequently arises from the quiet, disciplined work of hidden talent. These individuals consistently deliver results, solve problems before they escalate, and stabilise processes without drawing attention. The question for leaders is not merely to identify hidden talent but to structure teams and delegate responsibilities so that this talent multiplies productivity, enhances organisational intelligence, and drives sustainable success. Amplifying impact is about creating conditions in which silent achievers not only perform at their best but also enable others to excel, turning individual contributions into systemic advantage.

The first principle in amplifying impact is strategic team design. Teams must be structured not solely by hierarchy or formal authority, but by capability, relational influence, and complementary cognitive styles. Hidden talent often thrives when paired with colleagues who are extroverted, visible, or politically active, as this interplay balances visibility and substance. Leaders should assess not only what skills are needed but also how individuals interact, how informal influence flows, and how problem-solving capacity can be distributed across the team. An optimally designed team amplifies hidden talent rather than diluting it.

Consider an operations team in a global logistics company. One member, James, consistently identifies potential bottlenecks in the supply chain, while another, Priya, excels at negotiating with external vendors. James is highly effective but prefers to work quietly; Priya is visible and assertive by structuring the team so that James provides foresight and problem-solving. At the same time, Priya communicates solutions to stakeholders, the team amplifies impact: operational efficiency improves, relational influence is maximised, and each individual's strengths are leveraged without forcing uncomfortable visibility.

Delegation is the second critical lever. Leaders often delegate tasks but fail to delegate decision-making authority, particularly to hidden talent. Effective delegation for amplifying impact goes beyond assigning tasks; it involves entrusting individuals with responsibility, accountability, and the latitude to make decisions within defined boundaries. Hidden talent is highly motivated by autonomy and purpose. Thoughtful delegation allows them to operate at the top of their capacity, freeing leadership bandwidth while ensuring capable hands manage critical tasks.

Delegation requires clarity of purpose. Hidden achievers must understand not only what needs to be done but why it matters, what outcomes define success, and which constraints or parameters apply. Ambiguity undermines efficiency and increases cognitive load. By providing a clear framework, objectives, expected outcomes, and decision-making latitude, leaders empower hidden talent to act decisively while maintaining alignment with organisational priorities. This kind of delegation amplifies impact by multiplying operational capacity, accelerating problem-solving, and ensuring outcomes are both reliable and strategically aligned.

Another crucial element is role clarity and capability alignment. Hidden talent often possesses skills, relational influence, and problem-solving abilities that exceed those specified in their formal job description. Leaders should identify these capabilities and align responsibilities accordingly. Misalignment risks underutilisation or frustration; overextension risks burnout. Amplifying impact requires a nuanced understanding of individual strengths, potential, and capacity. Leaders who match responsibilities to capabilities enable hidden talent to operate at the intersection of skill and influence, generating results that exceed expectations.

Team dynamics must also be managed thoughtfully. Hidden talent often operates more effectively through relational influence than through formal authority. Leaders can amplify their impact by fostering environments in which collaboration is encouraged, knowledge is shared, and relational networks are recognised as vital levers of performance. By structuring teams to optimise these informal networks, organisations leverage the silent power of hidden talent to stabilise processes, accelerate problem-solving, and propagate knowledge organically.

Consider how informal networks operate in practice. At a financial services firm, analyst Lara has no formal authority but wields relational influence across multiple teams. She is consistently sought out for guidance, troubleshooting, and process advice. By structuring project teams to incorporate Lara's insights early in planning and decision-making, leaders amplify her impact: operational risks are mitigated, project timelines improve, and other team members are empowered to learn and act effectively. The result is not only enhanced performance but also a multiplier effect that extends well beyond her individual contribution.

Coaching and mentorship within teams further magnifies impact. Hidden talent thrives when supported to extend influence without visibility pressure. Leaders can facilitate coaching relationships in which experienced, silent achievers guide others in problem-solving, strategic thinking, and navigating organisational complexity. Mentorship in this context is subtle, relational, and focused on outcomes rather than recognition. It strengthens team capacity, embeds knowledge, and spreads expertise without forcing hidden talent into public-facing roles. Over time, this creates teams that are self-sustaining, resilient, and highly effective.

Decision-making structures are another lever for amplifying impact. Hidden talent often excels in foresight, scenario planning, and anticipating challenges. Organisations can design decision-making frameworks that allow these individuals to contribute strategically, even without formal authority. For example, including silent achievers in discussions on risk assessment, workflow optimisation, or process improvement ensures that decisions are informed by deep insight. Their input improves outcomes, reduces errors, and enhances organisational intelligence. This approach respects their preferred working style while harnessing their full potential.

Communication norms must be calibrated carefully. Hidden talent often prefers written, asynchronous, or small-group communication over public meetings. Leaders can structure team interactions to maximise engagement, clarity, and contribution. For instance, pre-meeting briefings, collaborative documentation, and small working groups allow silent achievers to contribute insightfully without the pressure of performative visibility. These practices not only enhance team decision-making but also maintain engagement and prevent disengagement or frustration from visibility pressure.

A critical principle in amplifying impact is layered delegation. Leaders can create cascading responsibility structures in which hidden talent takes ownership of specific domains and mentors and delegates to others within their purview. This approach scales their influence beyond individual tasks, allowing expertise and problem-solving approaches to propagate through the organisation. The multiplication effect of this strategy ensures that high-performing individuals drive outcomes that extend well beyond their immediate actions, embedding capability throughout the system.

Feedback mechanisms are essential to sustain performance, hidden talent benefits from precise, outcome-focused feedback rather than performative recognition. Leaders should provide regular, constructive feedback on results, problem-solving approaches, and influence within the team. Feedback should reinforce alignment with objectives, highlight areas of impact, and support development, while respecting the individual's preferred level of discretion. Well-structured feedback loops not only sustain engagement but also amplify impact by enhancing the effectiveness of hidden talent and those they influence.

Cross-functional deployment is another strategy. Hidden talent often possesses transferable skills and relational networks that extend beyond their immediate team. By structuring opportunities for cross-functional contribution, organisations multiply impact: expertise is shared, relational influence spreads, and problem-solving capacity scales. Leaders must ensure that these deployments respect autonomy, cognitive load, and motivation. When done thoughtfully, cross-functional exposure enhances organisational agility and leverages hidden talent as a force multiplier.

Team resilience is directly linked to the engagement and empowerment of hidden talent. Silent achievers frequently stabilise processes, anticipate bottlenecks, and resolve issues before they escalate. Leaders can amplify impact by identifying these individuals and positioning them where their stabilising influence is most needed. This requires understanding informal networks, workflow dependencies, and problem-solving patterns. By strategically deploying hidden talent, organisations not only prevent crises but also optimise team performance, ensuring that high standards are maintained under pressure.

Psychological safety is a foundational element in amplifying impact. Hidden talent thrives in environments where mistakes are treated as learning opportunities, ideas are welcomed, and contributions are respected, regardless of visibility. Leaders must foster psychological safety, enabling silent achievers to take initiative, experiment, and innovate without fear of public judgment. This not only enhances individual performance but multiplies team and organisational capacity by encouraging proactive problem-solving and knowledge sharing.

Another lever is recognition for outcomes, not visibility. While amplification requires influence, it does not require that hidden talent become performative. Recognition should highlight results, problem-solving, and relational influence rather than forcing public exposure. For example, acknowledging the stabilisation of a critical process in a team briefing, sending a private note of appreciation, or including their contributions in decision-making discussions amplifies impact without compromising discretion. Subtle recognition reinforces motivation, strengthens engagement, and signals that quiet achievement is valued strategically.

Scaling leadership influence is another dimension. Leaders who understand the multiplication effect of hidden talent can delegate authority in ways that extend their own influence. By empowering silent achievers to make decisions, mentor peers, and lead initiatives within defined domains, leaders extend the reach of organisational capacity without increasing managerial burden. This scaling effect ensures that decision-making, problem-solving, and innovation are distributed across the organisation rather than concentrated at the top, enhancing agility and responsiveness.

Consider a technology development team in which hidden talent comprises engineers who rarely present ideas in meetings but consistently produce solutions that resolve critical bugs. By structuring teams to allow these engineers to mentor junior staff, review code collaboratively, and guide technical decisions behind the scenes, the organisation multiplies productivity. Individual contributions become systemic, lessons learned propagate organically, and overall output improves, all without forcing public visibility. This exemplifies the core principle of amplifying impact: creating structures that enable quiet excellence to scale.

Continuous capability assessment is essential. Teams are dynamic; organisational priorities evolve; and the potential of hidden talent may grow into new domains. Leaders must monitor skill utilisation, engagement, and influence, adjusting team structure and delegation accordingly. Regular reflection ensures that hidden talent is not underutilised or overwhelmed, and that their contributions are consistently aligned with organisational objectives. By maintaining a dynamic understanding of capability and impact, leaders ensure that amplification is sustainable rather than episodic.

Knowledge transfer is a further multiplier. Hidden talent often possesses tacit knowledge and problem-solving heuristics that are not formally documented. Leaders can amplify organisational impact by structuring teams to facilitate knowledge sharing: pairing hidden achievers with peers, creating collaborative documentation practices, and embedding their approaches into standard workflows. This spreads expertise, enhances organisational learning, and ensures that critical knowledge is not lost or siloed.

Strategic project allocation also enhances amplification. Leaders can position hidden talent on high-leverage projects where their skills, foresight, and relational influence will have the most significant impact. Allocation should consider cognitive load, autonomy, and motivational alignment. By prioritising placement in initiatives that matter most to organisational outcomes, the influence of hidden talent is amplified, risk is mitigated, and organisational objectives are advanced efficiently.

Finally, amplifying impact requires a shift in leadership mindset. It is not enough to identify hidden talent; leaders must intentionally design structures, delegate authority, and create environments where quiet achievers can operate at scale. This mindset recognises that the loudest voice does not equate to the most significant impact; that influence without authority can drive outcomes more effectively than formal power; and that multiplying hidden talent is a strategic advantage that compounds over time.

Organisations that successfully amplify impact through hidden talent create systems that convert individual excellence into collective success. Silent achievers stabilise processes, accelerate problem-solving, mentor peers, and propagate expertise across teams. Teams are structured to maximise complementary strengths, minimise bottlenecks, and optimise relational networks. Delegation is thoughtful, autonomy is preserved, and recognition reinforces outcomes without demanding visibility. Knowledge is shared, influence is distributed, and organisational performance scales in ways that are both sustainable and strategic.

Amplification transforms hidden talent from isolated high performers into systemic multipliers. It converts individual insight into organisational intelligence, private excellence into collective achievement, and unseen contribution into visible results. Leaders who master this approach unlock exponential potential: the quiet problem-solvers, stabilisers, and innovators become engines of productivity, resilience, and strategic advantage.

In practice, amplifying impact means observing, intentionally designing, strategically delegating, and fostering environments that preserve autonomy, cognitive balance, and intrinsic motivation. It requires recognising relational influence, embedding knowledge transfer, facilitating mentorship, and positioning talent for maximum leverage. It is both an art and a science, combining human insight with structural strategy to create organisations that thrive on the power of hidden talent.

The ultimate lesson is clear: the loudest, most visible contributors are not always the most impactful. Hidden talent, when recognised, structured, and empowered thoughtfully, multiplies productivity, strengthens resilience, and drives sustainable organisational success. Amplifying impact is about creating conditions where excellence spreads quietly, influence propagates relationally, and contribution scales systemically. Leaders who embrace this principle unlock the most significant untapped advantage within their organisation, the invisible engine of achievement that consistently delivers results without spectacle.

Bringing Ideas Forward

Turning Hidden Insight into Organisational Impact

There is a particular kind of intelligence that hides itself, not out of shyness, not out of fear, and not because it doubts its own worth, but because it belongs to people who instinctively prioritise the work over the performance of the work. These are the quiet achievers; the ones whose minds gather insights the way still water gathers moonlight. Their ideas are often sharper, cleaner, and more considered than those offered in the loudest voices in the room, yet they hesitate to bring them forward. Not because they lack conviction but because they do not want to become entangled in the theatre of self-promotion that so often accompanies organisational life. They are not wired to posture. They do not chase visibility. Their integrity resists embellishment. And yet these are the people with the most original thinking, the clearest judgment, the most unfiltered understanding of how things really work. If organisations want to innovate with any real depth, they must find ways to help these quiet minds bring their ideas into the light, without forcing them to become what they are not.

This begins with understanding why their ideas often remain unspoken. Quiet achievers are typically not silent because they are disengaged or indifferent. They are silent because they are discerning. They think before they speak. They want to ensure their contribution is meaningful, not just noise. They want clarity, data, logic, and purpose. They refuse to talk for the sake of talking. And when they sense that a meeting is about performance, not substance, they withdraw, not out of insecurity but out of principle. They instinctively distinguish between a genuine conversation and a political one. And so, if leaders want to bring the ideas of quiet achievers forward, they must first create conditions in which contribution feels purposeful rather than performative.

The most significant barrier to innovation is not a lack of ideas but a culture that leads people to believe their ideas will be distorted, dismissed, misinterpreted, or politicised. Quiet achievers are particularly sensitive to this. They can feel when the room rewards bravado over thoughtfulness. They can sense when the decision has already been made, and contributions are merely a ritual. And they can immediately detect when a meeting is less about thinking and more about hierarchy theatre. In such environments, they do the rational thing, they keep their best ideas to themselves. Not out of malice, but out of efficiency. Why offer something precious if it will be mishandled?

But when leaders create environments where thinking is valued, where humility coexists with ambition, where the conversation feels like a genuine search for truth rather than a contest for dominance, quiet achievers come alive. They start speaking, not loudly, but clearly. Their ideas emerge not in a rush but in well-formed insights that shift the room. Their words carry weight because they are not inflated. They are distilled. And organisations that learn to distil this intelligence gain a competitive edge that cannot be replicated by noise.

Helping quiet achievers bring ideas forward is not about asking them to speak up more; it is about lowering the psychological cost of speaking. It means creating spaces where contribution feels natural rather than self-exposing. For many quiet thinkers, the traditional meeting is a hostile environment. Too fast. Too reactive. Too dominated by those who equate speed with intelligence. But quiet achievers think deeply. They process. They connect threads that others miss. They spot risks and possibilities long before the rest of the room catches up. And so, leaders must rethink how ideas enter the organisational bloodstream.

One of the most straightforward yet powerful strategies is to slow the early stages of discussion. Not everything needs to be answered immediately. Not every question deserves an immediate response. Sometimes the most intelligent contribution requires an evening, a walk, a night's sleep, or simply the time to think without interruption. When leaders create space for reflection, by inviting reflection before, after, or independently of meetings, they make a parallel channel of thought in which quiet achievers thrive. They enable them to contribute in a way that aligns with their cognitive strengths: deeply, calmly, and without the room noise drowning them out.

But slowing down is only part of the solution. Leaders must also expand the definition of contribution. Not all influence comes through speaking. Some of the most transformative ideas in organisations appear in documents quietly shared, models quietly refined, risks quietly mapped, and proposals quietly drafted after hours. These forms of contribution are often invisible in cultures obsessed with verbal performance. But leaders who understand the authentic architecture of innovation know that thinking happens everywhere, in careful writing, in diagrams, in asynchronous messages, in one-on-one conversations where the group noise no longer distorts the truth. They know that some of the best ideas surface when people have space to think privately before they are asked to think publicly.

The irony is that quiet achievers often have a more accurate understanding of the organisation than their louder counterparts. They see the informal networks. They sense the emotional undercurrents. They recognise the small inefficiencies that drain energy. They notice what's missing long before anyone else realises something is wrong. They observe patterns that most overlook because they do not spend their time signalling their own value. They spend it actually observing reality. And this observational intelligence becomes a deep reservoir of insight, one organisation cannot unlock unless they build pathways for these observations to be transformed into proposals, improvements, innovations, and influence.

One of the most overlooked tools in bringing quiet ideas forward is trust. Quiet achievers reveal their best thinking only when they trust the environment. Trust that their ideas won't be stolen. Trust that their contribution won't be dismissed. Trust that they won't be judged for how they speak but for what they say. Trust that the leader genuinely wants the truth, not validation. When trust exists, they offer ideas long before they are fully formed, knowing the leader will treat them with care. When trust doesn't exist, quiet achievers offer nothing, not out of defiance, but out of protection. They do not expose their ideas to environments that feel extractive or careless.

Trust is built not through grand gestures but through micro behaviours. A leader who listens without interrupting. A leader who asks, "What do you think?" and waits for the answer. A leader who admits they don't know everything. A leader who shares credit easily. A leader who gives quiet achievers autonomy because they know autonomy is what fuels their best work. A leader who does not dismiss an idea just because it wasn't delivered with confidence. These small behaviours accumulate, sending a powerful message: you can speak here, and what you say will be considered seriously.

Influence for quiet achievers cannot be built by imitating louder personalities. It must be built through depth. When quiet achievers contribute ideas that are clear, grounded, and thoughtful, they influence not by volume but by clarity. Their influence grows not because they dominate conversations but because they elevate them. Others begin to notice that when they speak, things make sense. When they contribute, decisions become wiser. Over time, their reputation becomes their influence. This influence is more substantial than that gained through charisma, as it is earned through integrity rather than performance.

But the real breakthrough occurs when organisations recognise that innovation is not a one-time event but a daily habit, one that must accommodate all cognitive styles, not just the loudest. Innovation is less about brainstorming sessions and more about the slow accumulation of small insights, tested and refined in quiet spaces. The best ideas often grow from conversations that begin cautiously and expand as the environment proves itself trustworthy. They emerge not from the pressure to perform but from the freedom to explore. Leaders who cultivate this freedom unlock what is perhaps the most underutilised asset in any organisation: the quiet mind capable of original thought.

Bringing ideas forward is also about removing the fear of being wrong. Quiet achievers are often more self-critical than others. They do not speak until they are certain. But innovation requires imperfection. It requires half-formed, raw, and unpolished ideas. When leaders model this, by freely offering imperfect ideas, they enable quiet achievers to do the same. They show that contribution is valued even before it is complete. And this subtle permission can open doors that loud encouragement never could.

Leaders can further support quiet innovators by creating structures that reduce the politics around ideas. Anonymous idea submissions. Rotating facilitation. Meetings where everyone writes ideas silently before anyone speaks. Sessions where speaking time is capped to prevent fast talkers from dominating. Debriefs where the quiet are invited to share their reflections afterwards. These structures convey that the organisation is not trying to force everyone into the same style, but rather to ensure that every style has a place to contribute.

But the most crucial strategy is this: leaders must protect the purity of ideas. Too often, ideas from quiet achievers are diluted by committees, dismissed by louder voices, or co-opted by those who want the credit without the work. When this occurs, quiet achievers quickly learn that it is safer to withhold their thinking. But when leaders guard their ideas, crediting them publicly, defending them privately, and ensuring they are evaluated on merit, the quiet step forward again. They test the environment using an alternative approach. Then another. And soon, the organisation has a steady flow of insights from minds that had previously remained unseen.

The future of innovation belongs not to the loudest but to the most thoughtful. As automation accelerates, as AI becomes more capable, as the superficial work of information processing becomes commoditised, the deepest ideas, the ones born of human judgement, empathy, intuition, and moral awareness, will come from the minds that think deeply, quietly, and without ego. These minds rarely demand attention, but they deserve it. They are the ones who will design the following systems, solve successive crises, and imagine the possibilities that follow. But only if leaders create a culture in which their contributions are not just allowed but actively sought.

Leadership, in this context, becomes an act of invitation. An invitation to think, to speak, to propose, to question, to imagine, to challenge. An invitation that says, "You do not need to perform to be valued here." Your ideas matter because you matter. Your way of thinking matters because it brings something no one else brings. Your quiet is not a limitation; it is an asset. It allows you to observe, process, connect, and understand. This understanding will move us forward.

Ultimately, bringing ideas forward is not about changing the quiet achievers, it is about changing the environment so the quiet achievers can change the organisation. It is about building cultures where ideas are judged by their merit, not by the volume of their delivery. It is about recognising that innovation is a collective act, not a performance. It is about trusting that the deepest minds often speak the softest. And it is about understanding that the future will be shaped not by those who shout the loudest, but by those who think the deepest, and are finally given the space to be heard.

Building a Culture that Sees

There is a quiet tragedy that plays out within organisations every day, and most leaders never notice it. It unfolds in meeting rooms where the loudest voice dominates the table while the most thoughtful one falls silent. It appears in performance reviews, where confidence is mistaken for competence and visibility is mistaken for value. It spreads in cultures where the people who work with quiet diligence go unrecognised because their brilliance is not wrapped in noise. And over time, a kind of organisational blindness sets in, leaders see what is obvious, not what is essential. The real work, the real intelligence, the real glue of the enterprise becomes invisible. Not because it isn't there, but because nobody has trained their eyes to look for it.

Building a culture that truly sees, one that rewards contribution over performance, depth over volume, quality over theatrics, is not a simple endeavour. It requires leaders to challenge the very instincts they've been praised for. It demands that organisations question the metrics they've relied on for decades. And it forces everyone, from the top down, to confront an uncomfortable truth: the way we recognise talent is often shaped by outdated ideas of what capability looks like. Cultures that celebrate noise usually overlook the quiet strengths that sustain them. Cultures that valorise self-promotion unintentionally punish humility. And cultures that equate confidence with competence end up advancing the wrong people while losing the ones who hold everything together.

To build a culture that sees, leaders must first confront the distorted lens through which they view people. Much of organisational life has become a theatre in which presentation matters more than substance. People have learned to be strategic with their visibility, curating how they appear rather than developing what they offer. They use bold slogans, adopt the language of leadership playbooks, and imitate the expected level of charisma. And because we've conditioned ourselves to believe that energy equals impact, we reward it, even when the energy carries little depth. Meanwhile, the quieter contributors, those who think before they speak, those who prefer solving problems to performing intelligence, those who only speak when something truly needs to be said, get overshadowed by the spectacle of it all. Not because they lack talent, but because their talent is expressed through restraint.

A culture that reverses this dynamic entirely. It is a culture where substance does not have to shout to be valued. Where contribution is measured not by how confidently it is delivered but by the integrity and impact it carries, where people are not forced into a mould of extroversion or self-promotion to be taken seriously. And where leaders take responsibility for looking beyond the obvious, knowing that the most transformative talent rarely walks into a room demanding attention.

The first shift leaders must make is in how they listen. Listening, in most organisations, has become reactive, something people do while waiting for their turn to speak. When leaders listen this way, they hear only the individuals who talk the most. Hidden talent, by its nature, does not compete for airtime. They do not rush to fill the silence. They do not fight for dominance. They speak when they have something grounded and meaningful to contribute. A leader trained only to recognise volume will miss them entirely. But a leader who listens with intention, not for performance, but for insight, will begin to notice the depth that often hides behind quietness. They will hear the competence that expresses itself without flair. They will recognise the calm, measured voice that anchors a chaotic discussion. This kind of listening is not passive; it is a discipline. It requires leaders to slow their instinct for rapid judgment, pay attention to substance beneath the surface, and value contributions based on clarity rather than charisma.

Another shift is needed in how leaders interpret behaviour. Hidden talent does not exhibit the characteristics of traditional high potentials. They do not self-promote, exaggerate achievements, chase credit, or posture for attention. Their impact is often indirect yet profound. They train others informally, stabilise teams quietly, resolve crises without ceremony, and uphold standards when others feel pressured to compromise. But because modern workplaces are wired to reward visibility over value, these behaviours often go unnoticed or undervalued. Leaders who fail to recognise this pattern frequently misinterpret humility as passivity, calmness as a lack of ambition, and steadiness as a lack of leadership potential. A culture that considers this thoroughly. It recognises that the traits most associated with hidden talent, integrity, discipline, consistency, and ownership, are the same as those required for sustainable success. Leaders understand that humility is not a lack of ambition but a sign of maturity; that calmness is not disengagement but emotional mastery; and that quietness is not a deficit but a deliberate choice to speak only when it matters.

Rewarding competence over noise requires leaders to rethink how they measure performance. Much of what organisations currently reward is performative: the ability to speak with confidence, to influence through personality, to appear decisive even when uncertain. Hidden talent does not invest in these performances, and so they often fall below leadership radars. Metrics must change. Instead of valuing speed, measure accuracy. Instead of celebrating visibility, measure reliability. Instead of praising big statements, measure follow-through. Instead of rewarding those who contribute the most words, reward those who contribute the most meaning. When performance is measured through these lenses, hidden talent rises naturally, not because they have changed, but because the system finally recognises the truth of their contribution.

A culture that also requires leaders to shift the power structures that define opportunity. Many organisations still operate on the assumption that talent reveals itself through ambition. Hidden talent does not push itself forward. Not because they lack ambition, but because they believe their work should speak for itself. In cultures that favour self-promotion, they remain invisible. To correct this, leaders must stop waiting for these individuals to raise their hands. Instead, they must actively seek them out. They must make it part of their leadership responsibility to identify the people who quietly drive the organisation. They must create pathways for advancement that do not rely on self-promotion but on demonstrated integrity, competence, and stewardship.

Opportunity cannot depend on who shouts the loudest; it must rely on who builds the most value for the enterprise.

Building a culture that also means examining the stories leadership tells about success. In many organisations, success is framed as a heroic narrative, bold risks, visible wins, charismatic leadership. This narrative is seductive, but incomplete. Most genuine success is built not on heroic moments but on consistent, unglamorous work done by people who ask for nothing in return. These individuals are rarely celebrated in company newsletters or leadership stories, but they are the ones who keep the organisation resilient. They are the ones who catch problems before they escalate, who maintain standards without applause, who act as the moral conscience of their teams. For a culture to see them, leaders must shift the narrative. They must celebrate not only the big wins but the quiet, everyday excellence that sustains the organisation. They must acknowledge the small acts of integrity that go unnoticed. They must tell stories that elevate contribution over performance, humility over bravado, consistency over theatrics. Culture is shaped by what leaders praise; when leaders praise quiet strengths, the organisation begins to recognise them as well.

One of the profound challenges in building such a culture is that it demands leaders hold themselves accountable in ways they may never have been asked to before. Leaders must confront their own biases, biases towards extroversion, confidence, charisma, and certainty. Biases that elevate style over substance. Biases that reward people who look the part rather than those who deliver the work. These biases run deep, often formed long before leaders entered their roles. Changing them requires humility, the willingness to admit that some of the people leaders have promoted were chosen not because they were the best, but because they were the easiest to recognise. It requires courage to shift from comfortable patterns to uncomfortable truths. It requires vigilance to ensure that the culture does not revert to old habits.

Leaders must also be willing to design systems that catch the invisible work. Hidden talent often entails emotional, relational, and intellectual labour that does not appear on performance dashboards. They are the ones colleagues consult for clarification. They are the ones teams rely on in times of uncertainty. They are the ones who protect morale, mentor new joiners, stabilise team dynamics, and uphold ethical standards. These contributions do not fit neatly into KPIs, but they are the backbone of team resilience. A culture that sees must find ways to formally acknowledge this labour, not with token appreciation, but with real recognition that shapes progression, reward, and opportunity.

Perhaps the most critical aspect of building a culture that sees is psychological safety, but not the oversimplified version often discussed in corporate rhetoric. Proper psychological safety is not about making everyone comfortable. It is about creating an environment where people can contribute without fear of being overlooked, dismissed, or overshadowed. Hidden talent thrives in environments where its depth is valued, its quietness is understood, and its integrity is seen as an asset rather than a hindrance. When leaders create spaces where introspective thinkers feel heard, reflective contributors feel respected, and cautious voices feel welcome, hidden talent naturally surfaces. They do not need to change who they are; they need an environment where who they are is recognised as valuable.

Building this kind of culture is slow, intentional work. It cannot be done through slogans or one-off workshops. It requires leaders to model the behaviour they wish to see. It requires them to demonstrate curiosity, ask more profound questions, reward honesty even when it complicates matters, invite diverse ways of thinking, and resist the allure of easy answers. Hidden talent reveals itself in cultures that honour effort as much as outcome, depth as much as confidence, honesty as much as ambition. When leaders genuinely demonstrate that they value these traits, not performatively, the organisation begins to shift.

Ultimately, building a culture that sees is not simply about fairness or morale. It is a strategic necessity. In a world where noise is easier to produce than substance, and visibility easier to perform than value, organisations risk losing the people who quietly hold everything together. Hidden talent is not fragile; it is discerning. When they feel unseen, they withdraw. When they feel misunderstood, they disengage. When they feel undervalued, they leave. And when they go, the organisation discovers, often too late, that it has lost something irreplaceable: the individuals whose work carried the trust, integrity, and resilience that no amount of noise can substitute.

A culture that sees does not emerge by accident. It is chosen, built, refined, and protected. It begins with leaders who decide that depth matters more than volume, that contributions matter more than performance, and that integrity matters more than showmanship. It continues with systems that recognise invisible work, metrics that reward genuine competence, narratives that honour quiet excellence, and environments in which deep thinking is not only allowed but expected. And it becomes sustainable when everyone, not just leaders, begins to internalise a different truth: that talent is not always obvious, that brilliance often hides in humility, and that the most valuable people in the organisation may be the ones who never seek attention.

The real test of whether a culture truly sees its people is what happens under pressure. Pressure exposes an organisation's DNA. Under pressure, leaders either narrow their focus to the most visible contributors or broaden their view to understand who is truly carrying the load. Hidden talent often emerges in these moments, not through grand gestures, but through steadiness. They do not panic when systems strain. They do not dramatise the difficulty. They anchor themselves and begin solving what is in front of them. They become the calm centre of the storm. And yet, in organisations where visibility is valued over depth, these moments are rarely attributed to them. Instead, credit gravitates upward or outward, towards those who narrate events more loudly rather than those who shaped them quietly. Leaders who wish to build cultures that see must reverse this gravitational pull. They must develop the discipline to trace the impact back to its trusted source. They must ask not who presented the outcome, but who created it. Not who communicated the success, but who enabled it. Not who spoke the loudest, but who held the responsibility. This is the only way to permanently shift the cultural bias that hides talent in plain sight.

But for a culture to truly see, leaders must also examine their relationship with discomfort. Hidden talent often brings uncomfortable truths to the surface. They are the ones who question flawed assumptions, highlight unspoken risks, and point out ethical dilemmas others would rather ignore. They are not inherently contrarian; they are loyal to the truth, and that loyalty makes them invaluable. But in cultures that reward harmony over honesty, these individuals are quietly punished. They become viewed as barriers rather than guardians. Leaders who are insecure or overly attached to their own narratives interpret their clarity as criticism. A culture that sees must become a culture that tolerates, even values, discomfort, the discomfort of deeper questioning, of confronting blind spots, of acknowledging weaknesses. Hidden talent thrives in such cultures because they recognise that critical thinking is not opposition; it is stewardship. They speak up not to undermine, but to protect the integrity of the work. Leaders who understand this begin to see that their role is not to avoid discomfort but to host it with maturity.

Recognition also plays a central role in building such a culture, but not in the superficial way often seen in companies today. Many organisations treat recognition as a performance: the monthly award, the spotlight announcement, the loud applause. These rituals usually reward the most visible contributions and unintentionally exclude those who do their best work quietly. Hidden talent does not crave public praise, but it does need to feel that someone sees its effort, understands its value, and respects its contribution. The most meaningful recognition is private, specific, and grounded in truth. It does not exaggerate achievements; it accurately names them. It does not flatter; it honours. When leaders offer this kind of recognition, honest, intimate acknowledgement of the work that truly matters, hidden talent gains something far more potent than applause: they gain trust. Trust is what encourages them to continue contributing at their highest level.

A culture that sees must protect against another subtle danger: the drift toward speed over wisdom. In a world obsessed with acceleration, organisations reward rapid responses, rapid decisions, and rapid pivots. But hidden talent does not rush the thinking process. They allow ideas to mature. They test assumptions before committing to them. They slow down precisely when the organisation is tempted to speed up. This patience is not hesitation; it is perspective. They know that a decision made too quickly is more likely to unravel later. When cultures treat reflection as inefficiency, hidden talent becomes misjudged as slow or overly cautious. But when cultures recognise that wisdom often requires space, the entire organisation benefits. Leaders must model this. They must show that thinking time is not wasted time, that depth is not the enemy of agility, and that long-term stability usually arises from short-term patience. Hidden talent does not need permission to think deeply; they need protection from the pace that punishes them for it.

Another vital dimension of building a culture that sees is reshaping how conflict is understood. Hidden talent rarely engages in unnecessary conflict but often holds strong internal standards. When they speak up, it is because something matters, not to them personally, but to the outcome or the ethics of the work. In cultures that avoid conflict, their contributions become muted. In cultures that lean too heavily into dominance, their voices are drowned out. A culture that sees must redefine conflict as a form of care. Honest disagreement is not dysfunction; it is the friction that polishes ideas. Leaders must create environments in which dissent is safe, questioning is welcome, and diverse perspectives strengthen decisions. Hidden talent contributes most powerfully when they feel their perspectives are not only tolerated but also valued. They bring clarity, nuance, and a kind of intellectual honesty that keeps organisations from drifting into complacency.

One of the most overlooked elements in building this culture is emotional literacy. Hidden talent often possesses a quiet emotional intelligence, they notice mood, tension, unspoken concerns, and subtle shifts in team dynamics. They sense when someone is overwhelmed before that person says anything. They step in with support before a problem becomes visible. They lead without a title through empathy rather than authority. But in emotionally blind cultures, this intelligence is neither valued nor recognised. Leaders who wish to create a culture that sees must become students of emotional nuance. They must learn to notice the unspoken, understand the weight of silence, and interpret the meaning behind behaviour that does not align with professional norms. Emotional literacy is not softness; it is precision. And cultures that cultivate it naturally elevate the individuals who embody it.

More than anything, building a culture that sees requires a fundamental redefinition of leadership. Leadership is not about being the most visible person in the room. It is not about having the most polished answers. It is not about projecting confidence or asserting control. Authentic leadership is the ability to recognise talent that does not announce itself. It is the discipline of observing quietly before acting loudly. It is the maturity to amplify voices that carry insight rather than volume. It is the humility to admit that the most critical intelligence in the room may not be the one speaking. Leaders who understand this shift from commanding attention to creating space. They design meetings where thinking is valued more than talking. They ask questions that elicit contributions from quieter contributors. They create rituals that make contributions easier for people who are uncomfortable on stage. They give credit to those who enable success, not only to those who narrate it. Leadership becomes not a performance but a responsibility.

When leaders start behaving this way, the culture begins to change at a cellular level. Teams become more balanced. Decision-making becomes more grounded. Innovation becomes more layered and less reactive. People feel safer bringing their whole selves forward, not only the polished parts but also the thoughtful, uncertain, deeply human parts of their intelligence. Hidden talent begins to rise not because they suddenly become louder, but because the culture finally becomes quieter. The noise recedes. The signal strengthens. Depth becomes visible.

Organisations often talk about "inclusive cultures," but inclusion without visibility is meaningless. Hidden talent does not want privilege, they want recognition. They seek an opportunity to contribute without performing. They want environments where thinking is valued, humility is recognised, effort is understood, and integrity is respected. And they want leaders who know that the people who matter most in an organisation are not always the ones who stand at the front, but often the ones who stand behind the work.

The final realisation for any leader committed to building a culture that sees is this: you cannot demand visibility from people you have not first made safe. Hidden talent does not emerge in environments where it feels exposed. They do not challenge norms in cultures where perceived consequences are severe. They do not step forward in systems where they believe their nature is a liability. When leaders create psychological safety rooted in respect, fairness, and curiosity, hidden talent does not need encouragement; it simply emerges. They share more. They lead informally. They contribute beyond their role. They solve deeper problems. They become cultural anchors.

And paradoxically, as the culture starts to see them, something else shifts: the entire organisation becomes more human. Not sentimental, not emotional in a chaotic way, but genuinely human. People stop competing for attention and begin focusing on contribution. Meetings shift from performance arenas to thinking spaces. Teams start to value accuracy over bravado, honesty over spin, and wisdom over confidence. The culture breathes. People feel a sense of permission to be real, not because authenticity is a slogan, but because depth is finally being rewarded.

Ultimately, building a culture that sees is not about changing people, it is about changing what the organisation notices. The talent has been there all along. The brilliance has always existed. The quiet strengths have always held the structure together. The only difference is that, finally, the culture has learned to see.

And perhaps this is the real test of any culture, not whether it can attract talent but whether it can genuinely see it once it arrives. Many organisations are excellent at noise management: they know how to celebrate visibility, amplify those who broadcast their own value, and reward those who move quickly in the corridors of perception. But when it comes to recognising substance, quiet, steady, competent, unshowy substance, they falter, because substance rarely steps forward to introduce itself. Hidden talent doesn't knock on the door. It is already inside, already doing the work, already solving the problem while others are still discussing it. And so, a culture that chooses to see must cultivate a different kind of lens, one that is attentive, observant, patient, and receptive. Leaders must become students of human contribution, not merely managers of human activity.

This shift is uncomfortable because it demands leaders change the very way they interpret value. In most organisations, value is measured in noise: presentations, airtime, visibility, self-promotion, confident stances in meetings, and strategic interruptions. But hidden talent rarely plays that game. Their value is recorded in quiet outcomes, not loud inputs. They seldom talk about the problem they solved because, to them, solving it was the point. They do not inflate their hours to signal effort because effort is not the currency that motivates them. They take ownership not because it wins credit but because ownership is what competent people do when something must be done well. If leaders want a culture that sees, they must re-anchor value in what truly matters: reliability, judgment, craft, self-sufficiency, and the rare ability to think without ego. This means rewarding outcomes over optics, dignity over drama, and contribution over self-promotion. It means leaders must train themselves to look beyond the performance of confidence and evaluate the substance of their contributions.

What makes this shift particularly challenging is that modern workplaces have grown accustomed to performance cultures rather than competence cultures. A performance culture is one in which people become fluent at appearing effective. They can discuss strategy, demonstrate credibility, and craft compelling narratives about their work. But competence cultures reward those who actually deliver, irrespective of how quietly. Competence cultures are quieter but infinitely more stable. They produce fewer shocks, fewer crises, and fewer last-minute scrambles because, beneath the surface, a network of people takes their responsibilities seriously. These individuals rarely seek recognition, but they always deserve it. And when a leader finally begins to see them, the organisation's emotional climate changes.

Because there is something deeply human about being seen. Not applauded, not spotlighted, not given a performative badge of honour, seen. When hidden talent is seen, even subtly, their shoulders lift in ways they didn't know they had lowered. They feel a quiet dignity, a sense that their integrity has been recognised without them needing to advertise it. And this dignified recognition creates a ripple effect across teams. The loudest voices lose their monopoly on influence. The quieter ones feel psychologically safe enough to contribute more openly. Meetings become richer because the thinking deepens rather than merely intensifies. People start listening again. The wind shifts, almost imperceptibly at first, and then unmistakably, until the culture breathes differently.

The leader who creates this kind of culture is doing something profoundly countercultural. They are choosing depth over speed, truth over performance, groundedness over optics. They are rejecting the easy lure of visible effort and instead seeking the quieter patterns beneath the surface. They are choosing to elevate the people who elevate the organisation. And this choice is not soft, sentimental, or idealistic, it is strategically brilliant. The organisations that endure are not built on charisma but on competence. They survive turbulence because they have people who remain steady. They innovate responsibly because they have people who think before they move. They grow sustainably because they have people who understand that integrity is not an optional accessory but the operating system of absolute excellence.

But if leaders want to build this culture, they must confront one of the most stubborn obstacles in modern workplaces: the myth that confidence equals competence. It doesn't. It never has. However, organisations are consistently fooled by this illusion because confidence is visible, whereas competence is often invisible. Confidence speaks in headlines; competence works in footnotes. Confidence fills the air; competence fills the gaps. And the irony is that organisations continue to reward those who perform certainty rather than those who quietly construct the foundation beneath it. A leader who wants a culture that sees must develop an almost forensic sensitivity to this difference. They must learn to ask: Who is actually doing the work? Who is thinking clearly? Who is solving the problems when no one is watching? Who brings the room back to sanity when everyone else is panicking? Who can be trusted when things go wrong? Those questions reveal the hidden pillars of an organisation, and once identified, those pillars must be honoured.

Honouring hidden talent does not always mean promoting them in the traditional sense. In fact, many do not crave title, hierarchy, or spotlight. They crave fairness, respect, meaningful work, a leader who notices, and the freedom to deliver well without being micromanaged. They seek environments in which competence is not merely helpful but celebrated. Even though they do not seek recognition, leaders must ensure recognition finds them. This can be subtle, an acknowledgement in a conversation, a trusted role in a complex project, an invitation into a space usually reserved for louder voices. This private comment says, 'I see what you did there. Thank you.' These small, meaningful gestures matter far more to hidden talent than any public theatrics. They are signals that the culture is paying attention. Over time, these signals accumulate and form the scaffolding of a workplace where the quiet thrive.

But seeing hidden talent is only half the work. Leaders must also design the environment so that louder, more assertive personalities do not overshadow hidden talent. This entails rethinking how meetings are conducted, how decisions are made, how feedback is communicated, and how credit is distributed. Too often, the loudest person in the room is assumed to be the most knowledgeable, simply because they occupy the most sonic space. But leaders can break that pattern by deliberately slowing conversations, inviting quieter voices to speak first, ensuring everyone has the psychological safety to share dissenting views, and modelling deep listening. When leaders demonstrate that thoughtful input matters more than forceful delivery, the culture recalibrates naturally.

Reward systems must change, too. Cultures that often see their metrics shift from hours logged to outcomes delivered, from performance in meetings to consistency in execution, from visibility to impact. This requires courage because visibility is easy to measure, while impact is not. Impact hides inside systems, relationships, silent problem-solving, avoided crises, and the unseen labour that keeps organisations standing. But when leaders start assessing impact, they inevitably discover a trove of talent that has been sitting unnoticed. The quiet person who resolves conflicts before anyone else hears about them. The analyst who spots a risk months before it materialises. The operations person who turns chaos into order without fanfare. The engineer who fixes something permanently, so the organisation no longer wastes time on the same recurring issue. The administrator who may not speak much but whose organisational intelligence runs through the entire team. These contributions rarely appear on dashboards, yet they save companies millions, stabilise teams, and safeguard reputations.

A culture that also requires leaders to remove cultural noise, behaviours that distort perception of value. Cultural noise includes grandstanding, performative stress, political manoeuvring, strategic complaining, intellectual bullying, jargon masquerading as depth, and the insidious habit of taking credit for others' work. When these behaviours remain unchecked, hidden talent withdraws. They don't quit immediately; they retreat into necessity. They stop offering more than required. They do not volunteer ideas. They do not push boundaries. They do not challenge flawed thinking. They survive. Survival mode is detrimental to creativity, loyalty, and innovation. But when leaders actively silence cultural noise, hidden talent begins to re-emerge. They test the environment with small contributions. They risk offering ideas. They gradually trust that the culture is safe enough for them to bring their whole selves. And once they do, the organisation's energy changes.

What makes hidden talent so transformative is not merely their competence but their character. They possess an internal compass that cannot be taught, along with integrity, ownership, thoughtfulness, humility, responsibility, and self-regulation. These qualities form the emotional backbone of a strong organisation.

They are the people who stay calm when pressure rises, who think clearly when others react, who hold the line when standards slip, who keep the mission steady when politics swirl around them. They are the ones you want beside you when everything goes wrong. And this is why cultures that see do not just improve performance, they improve resilience. They become more stable, less susceptible to drama, and better able to weather uncertainty. Hidden talent does not just perform tasks; they also strengthen the organisation's emotional architecture.

But even with all this, leaders must recognise a final truth: seeing hidden talent is not a static achievement but a continuous discipline. People change. Cultures drift. Noise creeps back in, systems decay. And so, leaders must cultivate an almost meditative attentiveness to the human landscape. They must observe not only what people say but what they actually do. They must watch for the quiet contributors, the subtle collaborators, the unnoticed mentors, the people who make others better simply by being present. They must create rituals of observation: moments where they step back from the noise and ask, 'Who is truly holding this place together?' Leadership, at its best, is the art of noticing.

And when an entire culture learns to notice, something remarkable happens: hidden talent becomes less hidden. Not because it becomes louder, but because the culture becomes wiser. People start recognising competence in others. They begin to value the work that often goes unseen. They learn to appreciate the quiet heroes in their teams. They redistribute attention. They recalibrate influence. They give space to people who previously worked in the shadows. As a result, the organisation becomes more cohesive. It becomes a place where people need not compete for recognition because recognition is grounded in truth. It becomes a place where value is not assigned by volume but by integrity. It becomes a place where people can breathe.

The irony is that when you build a culture that sees, you also attract more hidden talent. They find you because they recognise environments in which they will be safe, respected, and able to craft meaningful work. Hidden talent is not drawn to flashy benefits or slogans about culture plastered across walls. They are drawn to quiet competence, to steady leadership, to environments where drama is optional rather than compulsory. They are drawn to places where they can get on with making things excellent. Once they gather, the organisation shifts from operating on noise to operating on depth.

This is the long game of leadership. Not the game of quick wins or visible theatrics, but the game of constructing an environment where the strongest people thrive, and the real work gets done. It is a game built on patience, humility, curiosity, and the willingness to question long-held assumptions about how value appears. It is a game for leaders who are tired of shallowness and hungry for substance. Leaders who are ready to build organisations that last, not because they are loud, but because they are grounded in the kind of human quality that no technology, no automation, no trend, no disruption can replace.

A culture that sees is not built overnight. It is built conversation by conversation, decision by decision, moment by moment. It is built every time a leader chooses to listen deeply rather than react quickly. It is built every time a leader resists the temptation to reward noise and instead honours real contribution. It is built every time someone quietly competent realises that, finally, someone has noticed.

And once a culture becomes capable of seeing, it becomes capable of something even more powerful: becoming a place where people grow into the fullness of who they can be. Hidden talent does not remain secret forever when provided with the right environment. It blossoms. It takes shape. It steps forward, not loudly, but meaningfully. It becomes a source of wisdom, stability, and excellence that sustains the organisation long after the noise has passed. And this, in the end, is the quiet revolution available to every leader: build a culture that sees, and you will uncover the treasure that was there all along.

SECTION V

LEADERSHIP RESPONSIBILITY

What leaders must become

Your Role as a Leader

Leadership, when you strip away the noise, is not really about strategy decks, grand speeches, or the illusion of control. It is, at its heart, the art of noticing. Noticing what others miss, seeing what people are too busy, too distracted, or too self-important to pay attention to. Noticing the almost invisible currents of capability running beneath the surface of your organisation. Noticing the quiet ones. The unpolished ones. The ones who do not clamber for your attention, but who, if you were to stop, slow down, and look properly, might carry more potential than anyone else in the room. Your role as a leader in a rapidly changing world is shifting. It is no longer enough to be the one who sets the vision, marshals resources, and proves their worth through volume, visibility, or velocity. The next era of leadership belongs to those with the wisdom to find strength in silence, value in modesty, and genius in places others overlook. It belongs to leaders capable of building organisations that are not merely efficient, but alive, alive with hidden capability, quiet brilliance, the sort of grounded competence that makes the impossible suddenly look strangely manageable.

For too long, leadership has been shaped by a deeply flawed assumption: that those who shine brightest publicly are those who shine strongest privately. That confidence equals competence. That visibility equals value. But you already know that this is not true. You know it because you've worked in organisations where the loudest voices won the room but lost the plot. You've seen meetings where decisions were driven by ego rather than substance. You've watched talented people quietly pick up the pieces after someone else claimed the credit. And you've probably felt, at least once, the frustration of knowing that the real experts weren't in the conversation because they didn't push themselves forward in the "acceptable" way. The future of leadership demands that we break with those assumptions. Because the organisations that will win in this new age, the age of hybrid intelligence, shifting workforce expectations, and the collapse of old hierarchies, are those led by people willing to see beyond the obvious. People are eager to dig deeper. People are willing to notice.

Hidden talent is not a mystical concept. It is simply talent misaligned with systems designed for a different kind of person. Businesses, for decades, rewarded charisma, assertiveness, and a very narrow definition of leadership presence. But as work becomes more complex, more interdisciplinary, more emotionally intelligent, and more reliant on psychological safety, that old model is crumbling. The quiet thinker who can hold contradictions without panic; the calm operator who executes under pressure without applause; the introverted analyst whose subtle pattern recognition saves millions; the thoughtful communicator who brings clarity to chaos; the conscientious implementer who delivers excellence again and again without needing an audience, these are the people the next generation of leaders must learn to see. And to see them, leaders will have to change. Not in a shallow, cosmetic way. But in a deep, fundamental way. In how they listen, evaluate, build trust, create space, reward, design their teams, check their instincts, and even define success.

You cannot identify hidden talent if your leadership identity is built on being the centre of attention. You cannot nurture hidden talent if you equate silence with weakness. You cannot retain hidden talent if you reward noise over nuance. And you cannot claim to be a modern leader if you still cling to the outdated belief that leadership means being the loudest, busiest person in every conversation. There is a different path. One grounded in humility, curiosity, and the courage to relinquish control. One in which leadership is not a performance but a responsibility. One where the highest authority in the room is not the person who speaks most fluently, but the one who listens most deeply.

Imagine, for a moment, that your organisation is a large boat, not a sleek racing yacht, but a vessel designed for long journeys across unpredictable seas. Many leaders stand proudly on the bow, hair in the wind, imagining themselves steering the future. Below deck, however, is where the real work happens. The people maintaining the engine, adjusting the ballast, navigating by instrument, balancing fuel, repairing leaks, and anticipating storms. You may never hear their voices above the sound of the wind, waves, and ceremony. But they are keeping you afloat. And here is the uncomfortable truth: in many organisations today, the captain does not know the names of the people saving the boat. They know, instead, the loud ones on deck, the ones whose job is to look useful rather than be useful. They know the talkers, not the doers. They see the spotlight, not the shadow. And when the world was calm, perhaps that was enough. But the seas are no longer quiet. The waters are shifting too fast. The storms come too suddenly. The complexity of navigation has outgrown the old ways of working. If you, as a leader, do not learn to go below deck and truly see the people keeping the vessel alive, you will lose them. And when they go, your organisation will begin to take on water long before you realise why.

Your call to action is simple, but not easy: you must become a leader who can see the whole boat.

This begins with your eyes. Not the literal eyes that scan emails or board papers, but the inner eyes that observe patterns, energy, courage, and potential. Those who excel quietly rarely self-identify. They won't knock on your door to announce their brilliance. They won't ask for a promotion until they've proven themselves six times over. They won't interrupt a meeting to correct someone's flawed thinking. They won't tell you they're burned out. They won't parade their achievements because they see achievement as the natural outcome of doing a job properly, not as currency for negotiation. To find them, you must pay attention to the subtle signs: the calm voice in a crisis, the consistent delivery when others flounder, the insightful question that shifts the whole room, the colleague everyone trusts but no one spots, the person who listens fully before speaking, the one who never makes it about them. Hidden talent leaves traces. You need to know where to look.

Your next role is to create an environment where this kind of talent can breathe. Psychological safety is not a cliché; it is a structural necessity. Hidden talent thrives when there is space for authenticity, when humility is not punished, and when contribution is valued over performance. This entails accommodating different communication styles, thinking patterns, and confidence levels. It means gently rebalancing meeting dynamics so that the loudest voices do not dominate by default. It means noticing who has ideas but not airtime. It means encouraging reflection rather than demanding instant responses. It means designing work, so it does not assume everyone thinks aloud or processes information socially. The leaders who win the future will be those who can create ecosystems, not echo chambers.

Empathy becomes your operating system. Not the soft, sentimental empathy that many associate with "being nice", but a deep, disciplined empathy, the kind that allows you to understand what motivates someone, how they work, where they flourish, what they fear, and how they grow. If you want to nurture hidden talent, you must build trust long before you need it. Noticing is the first step; believing is the second. Many people with extraordinary ability have spent their entire careers being underestimated. When you finally see them, they might struggle to see themselves. They may hesitate to step into the light because the light has seldom been safe for them. Encouragement, when it is sincere and specific, becomes an act of liberation. A few carefully placed words from a leader, "I see what you're doing, and it's exceptional", can unlock years of stalled potential.

But the fundamental transformation comes from alignment. Hidden talent does not need rescuing; it needs direction. When people are placed in roles that match their strengths, when their working patterns are respected rather than corrected, when their contributions are recognised rather than appropriated, their performance doesn't merely improve, it compounds. This is the quiet magic of proper career pathing. It is not about pushing people up a ladder they never asked to climb. It is about shaping paths around who they are, not who the organisation assumes they should be. It is about unlocking their capacity to excel without requiring them to mimic another's leadership style. Not everyone wants to lead teams. Not everyone wants a bigger title. Not everyone wants to be visible. But everyone wants to feel their work matters. Everyone wants to belong. Everyone wants a leader who sees them clearly.

Your role, then, is not to manufacture more leaders. It is to cultivate more impact. And impact takes many forms. Some people's brilliance is best expressed in strategy. Others in execution. Others in analysis, operations, mentoring, problem-solving, or stabilising a team's emotional climate. Your job is to recognise this diversity of contribution and elevate it, rather than forcing everyone through the same narrow funnel. This requires a broad perspective, humility toward ego, and patience in practice. It requires you to question your organisation's default settings. Why are some behaviours rewarded? Why are some ignored? What assumptions underpin your definitions of potential, performance, or readiness? Whose voices are not heard? Who never feels comfortable speaking up? Who hides their capability behind modesty because that is how they were raised, conditioned, or protected? Who is quietly holding the team together without recognition? If you do not interrogate these patterns, your future will be built on the wrong foundations.

And here is the truth many leaders avoid: you cannot transform your organisation until you transform your habits. It is not enough to admire the idea of hidden talent. You must build routines that reveal it. That means regularly stepping out of your usual circles and spending time with people several layers removed from you. It means scheduled listening, not performative town halls, but honest, intentional conversations. It means being curious without an agenda. It means asking not, "What have you done?" but "What are you capable of that we haven't seen yet?" It means observing not only what people say but also the quality of their thinking. It means doing the unglamorous work of enquiry, reflection, and recalibration. Leadership, in this age, is less about steering the ship and more about understanding the boat well enough that the whole crew can steer with you.

It also requires courage. Because once you begin to see hidden talent, you may realise something unsettling: some of the people currently in positions of influence do not deserve to be there. Some have built their authority on volume rather than value. Some rely on politics rather than performance. Some have mastered the art of visibility while outsourcing the real work to others. And you, as a leader, will face a choice. Do you protect the old order because it is familiar, or do you build a new one because it is right? Transformative leadership is not passive. It is not polite. It is not appeasing. It requires you to challenge entrenched behaviours, redesign systems, and confront brutal truths about your culture. It requires you to elevate those who have earned influence and gently diminish those who have relied on theatrics. This is the real work. It is not glamorous, but it is essential.

And when you do this, when you create an organisation where hidden talent is not hidden anymore, something extraordinary happens. The atmosphere changes, the energy shifts. Meetings become richer. Execution becomes cleaner. Innovation becomes more grounded. Collaboration becomes more real. The culture becomes more humane. People feel safe, seen, and valued. They give more not because they are asked to, but because they want to. And that is how organisations move from fragile to resilient, from good to great, from drifting to purposeful. The captain begins to understand the boat. The people below deck rise to the deck. The vessel moves faster, steadier, and farther than anyone expected.

Your legacy as a leader will not be measured by the size of your title or the sharpness of your strategy. It will be measured by how many people grew because of you. How many careers accelerated because you cared enough to look closely? How many brilliant, quiet people found the confidence to step forward because you held open the space? How many futures were shaped because you chose to lead differently? This is the impact that lasts. Not the quarterly numbers. Not the applause at awards dinners. But the transformation you ignite in people who barely knew they were capable of becoming something greater.

And so, here is the invitation, your call to action. It is not dramatic. It is not ceremonial. It is not a rallying cry in the style of corporate manifestos. It is simpler, but far more powerful: start paying attention. Pay attention to the people who deliver without spectacle. Pay attention to the potential that hides behind humility. Pay attention to the talent buried beneath old assumptions. Monitor the energy shifts in a room. Pay attention to the ones others overlook. Pay attention to the quiet ones with extraordinary edges. Pay attention to anything that feels steady, grounded, and sincere. Pay attention to what makes your organisation truly work.

From there, commit. Commit to changing how you listen. Commit to redesigning your talent assessment process. Commit to challenging your own biases. Commit to giving space to the people who would never take it for themselves. Commit to creating careers, not just filling roles. Commit to identifying the talent that may never self-advocate. Commit to building a culture where no one needs to be loud to be seen. Commit to becoming the kind of leader people remember for the right reasons.

Ultimately, leadership is stewardship. You are the guardian of potential. The custodian of culture. The architect of opportunity. The one who decides whether brilliance flourishes or withers. The one who decides whether the quiet ones are lost or found. The one who shapes whether your organisation survives the future or is overtaken by it.

And if you choose differently, if you decide to lead with humility, curiosity, and courage, then you will not just find hidden talent. You will unleash it. You will cultivate a depth of capability that transforms your teams, your culture, your performance, and even your own sense of purpose.

Your role as a leader is not to shine alone. It is to serve as a guide for others.

And the journey begins the moment you choose to look where others never do.

Building Teams of Depth

Building teams of depth begins with a different way of seeing, because most organisations are still structured around what is easily measured rather than what is truly valuable. Titles, job descriptions, and loud contributions all sit above the waterline like the visible tip of an iceberg. Still, the mass beneath the quiet capability, the trusted problem-solvers, the hidden connectors carry the weight of real organisational resilience. The challenge for modern leaders is not simply to manage teams efficiently, but to design environments in which this submerged strength is recognised, nurtured, and integrated into the core of how the team thinks, moves, and succeeds. Hidden talent has always existed. Every organisation you walk into has people who carry far more than they are credited for: the person who knows why a legacy system keeps failing and how to coax it back to life, the colleague who quietly rebuilds trust between teams, the meticulous thinker who rewrites a process in a way that saves countless hours, the calm human anchor who steadies a group in moments of crisis. The problem is not the absence of such people, it is that leaders rarely build systems that allow them to shine without having to shout, politic, self-promote or reshape their personalities to fit a certain managerial template. We have built cultures that reward noise over nuance, and then wonder why our organisations struggle to innovate, transfer knowledge, or retain the people we depend on most. Depth, therefore, begins with attention. Not the performative attention of formal reviews or talent grids, but the softer, observational kind: noticing who people go to when something breaks; noticing who quietly prepares for meetings by stitching disparate pieces together; noticing whose name is mentioned with relief rather than fanfare. Designing deep teams requires leaders who treat these observations not as anecdotes but as data. And once you start observing closely, you inevitably see the gap between the org chart and the real organisation. The org chart is a fiction, tidy, linear, hierarchical. The real organisation is a web of conversations, shared memory, informal influence and unspoken dependency. Some of the most influential people are nowhere near the top of the hierarchy; they sit at the crossroads of knowledge. Integrating hidden talent starts by acknowledging that the value someone adds is often unrelated to their job title. Yet seeing is not enough. You must create an environment where deep contributions are not only possible but also protected. Modern work is hostile to depth. The endless meetings, sprint reviews, and shallow notifications, these not only reduce productivity; they actively prevent people from entering the cognitive state required to produce meaningful thought. Hidden talent often carries the kind of thinking that requires immersion: solving a system-level failure, redesigning a broken process, constructing a narrative bridge across organisational silos. Those tasks cannot be done in ten-minute intervals carved between calendar clutter. Teams of depth are built by leaders who understand that focus is strategy. Protecting deep time is not a perk; it is a cultural signal: here, thinking is valued. Here, reflection is not laziness. Here, spaciousness is a form of respect. And once people feel that respect, they contribute differently. They bring the full breadth of their ability, not just the fraction they can squeeze between distractions. They take intellectual risks. They follow threads that lead to breakthroughs. They connect dots no one else saw. When leaders protect time, they protect potential. But depth is not solely an individual matter. It is also relational. Hidden talent flourishes in psychological safety, not because they are fragile, but because deep work is inherently vulnerable. Offering a new idea, to reveal a concern others missed, or asking a question that exposes a blind spot requires courage. Quiet contributors think carefully before speaking because they care deeply about precision, not because they lack conviction. In an unsafe environment, they withdraw, not out of weakness but out of discernment. They know the cost of being misunderstood, dismissed or politicised. Safe environments allow depth to surface because they separate the person from the idea. They allow debate to be a form of respect rather than a form of combat. They enable people to say, "I don't know yet, but I think there's something here," without fearing reputational cost. And when you create that kind of climate, you discover that the people with the most valuable thoughts are often not the ones who rush to speak but the ones who wait until it matters. Teams of depth require an architecture as well. They need roles that legitimise invisible labour. Most hidden contributors work in roles that do not fully describe their work. They are unofficial integrators, translators, mentors, and custodians of organisational memory. They prevent failures that would cost millions, but because failures never occur, their value is invisible. Teams designed for depth acknowledge these invisible responsibilities by naming them, resourcing them, and distributing them fairly. When you formally recognise someone as a system steward or knowledge integrator, you not only honour their contribution but also reduce the risk of burnout. Recognition becomes a structural act rather than a sentimental one. And that matters because the politics of recognition remain one of the most corrosive forces in organisations. The people who keep teams alive do not always generate the glamorous metrics. They are the ones who listen, who test assumptions, who prevent unnecessary escalation. If you reward only the loud, you end up with brittle teams, teams that look strong from a distance but collapse under pressure. Rewarding depth requires tools that capture nuance: narrative feedback rather than tick-boxes, peer nominations rather than self-reporting, career paths that honour stewardship rather than just upward mobility. A team of depth is one in which the value of contribution is not reduced to the volume of voice. Another critical element is mobility. Hidden talent withers when trapped. When someone has deep, unusual capability, you want to give them a stretch without exposing them to politics or overwhelming them with work. Internal mobility, short projects, cross-functional pods, problem-solving missions, lets people test new capacities safely. It reveals unexpected combinations of skill. It creates redundancy, thereby reducing the organisation's dependence on a single silent hero. And importantly, it signals trust: we see what you can do, and we want more of it. That sense of being seen is often what keeps hidden talent committed. Leaders often ask why their most dependable people suddenly leave. The answer is rarely dramatic. It is usually a slow attrition of meaning: feeling overlooked, taken for granted, and permanently burdened, yet rarely uplifted. Teams of depth prevent this by building a continuous loop of contribution, recognition, replenishment and growth, a healthy ecosystem rather than an extractive one. Designing teams this way requires a mindset shift: depth is not efficiency. It is not the fastest output. It is not the most visible short-term result. Depth is sustainability. It is the difference between teams that can handle complexity and teams that shatter at the first unexpected problem. It is the difference between organisations that adapt and those that defend the past until it becomes fatal. And perhaps most importantly, building teams of depth is an ethical choice. To integrate hidden talent is to honour the dignity of contribution. It is to say: your value is not determined by how loudly you speak or how neatly your work fits a category. Your value is in the way you think, the way you hold the team together, the way you solve problems others cannot see, the way you bring quiet excellence to the table. When organisations adopt this view, they stop treating people as interchangeable units and start treating them as unique contributors to a shared endeavour. Building teams of depth is ultimately an act of leadership maturity. It requires humility, because you must admit that you do not yet see all the talent you rely on. It requires courage, because you must redesign systems that favour the familiar. It requires patience, because depth grows slowly, like roots strengthening beneath the surface. But if you commit to it, the payoff is extraordinary. You get teams that not only perform but also endure. Teams that hold each other accountable without fear. Teams that innovate without chaos. Teams where the quietest people often become the anchors, the navigators, the guardians of quality. And in a world obsessed with speed, surface and noise, organisations with actual depth become rare and magnetic. They attract people who crave meaning. They retain people who want to build something that lasts. They develop a steady, reliable momentum that allows them to navigate volatility with steadiness and intelligence. To build teams of depth is to build for the long term. It is to design not just for output but for wisdom. It is to create organisations that do not collapse when the loudest voice leaves the room. Ultimately, it is to recognise a simple truth: sustainable success is never built on the surface. It is built in the quiet, patient, brilliant work of people who were always there, you just needed to learn how to see them.

SECTION VI

TECHNOLOGY, AI, AND THE FUTURE

Why hidden talent matters more than ever

Technology, AI, and the Human Edge

In the era we find ourselves in, an era humming with algorithmic certainty and automation that never sleeps, there's a growing belief that technology is becoming the great leveller of human capability. Machines now perform tasks once reserved for specialists in seconds; knowledge that once took years to accumulate is retrievable with a few keystrokes; decisions that once demanded long, quiet thought is now offered as recommendations by systems designed to optimise everything from workflows to worldviews. And yet, quietly, almost stubbornly, something deeply human continues to stand apart. Something that technology cannot quite touch, cannot quite imitate, cannot quite decode. It is the quiet, unpolished, unadvertised strength of hidden talent. And in this new age of automation, its value is not diminishing, it is hardening into the very edge that organisations will rely on for survival.

Because as much as we talk about artificial intelligence replacing work, the truth is far more nuanced: AI automates the obvious; hidden talent safeguards the essential. AI runs tasks; hidden talent holds the line. AI predicts patterns; hidden talent evaluates meaning. AI executes; hidden talent owns outcomes. This isn't nostalgia for a pre-digital world, it is recognition of what machines are not designed to carry: integrity, judgement, courage, discernment, and the willingness to stay in the problem long enough to understand what is truly at stake. Hidden talent embodies these qualities not because they are trained to do so, but because something in their nature naturally bends toward responsibility rather than exposure, toward contribution rather than visibility, toward truth rather than ease. And when technology becomes the new infrastructure of organisational life, these are the individuals who quietly ensure that the system does not drift from its purpose, its ethics, or its humanity.

Anyone who has ever worked alongside hidden talent knows this instinctively. They are the ones who stay calm when everything else becomes chaotic, not because they're unemotional, but because they intuitively separate noise from signal. They are the ones who call out risks long before dashboards flash red, not from pessimism but from realism grounded in experience. They are the ones who resist shortcuts when integrity is at stake, even when no one would notice the difference. They recognise that automation is powerful. Still, context is everything, that no algorithm, no matter how sophisticated, truly understands the weight of a promise, the texture of a relationship, or the fallout of a misjudgement. These are the people AI will never replace, because AI cannot replicate character.

As automation increases, organisations often assume their competitive advantage will come from adopting more tools, systems, and machine-led decision-making mechanisms. However, the real advantage lies in understanding the boundaries of those tools. AI is extraordinary at scaling tasks; it is terrible at understanding consequences. It is brilliant at analysing past patterns; it has no instinct for moral cost. It can optimise processes; it cannot defend principles. And so, we edge into a paradox: the more technologically advanced an organisation becomes, the more dependent it is on the steady, grounded, deeply human judgement of hidden talent. They become the conscience of the digital enterprise, the load-bearing beam that holds the structure when the system becomes too complex, too ambiguous, too unpredictable for automation to navigate alone.

The irony is that these people rarely put themselves forward. In a world saturated with loudness, they remain the quiet ones. While others make sweeping statements about AI, they are the ones who question assumptions, ask what happens when the model fails, and point out ethical blind spots. They don't do this to prove intelligence; they do it to protect the integrity of the work. And it is here that the human edge becomes evident as technology becomes the dominant force in workplaces. AI can surface data, but it takes human depth to interpret it honestly. AI can propose solutions, but it takes human courage to choose the right one. AI can highlight anomalies, but it takes human intuition to detect when something is off, even when the numbers appear clean. AI can support decisions, but it cannot make judgments worthy of trust.

Trust is the operative word. Trust is the currency that will matter more than speed, efficiency, or scale. And trust, unlike data, cannot be automated. You trust people because you see their consistency under pressure. You trust them because they show up when it matters. You trust them because you've watched them make difficult choices without fanfare. You trust them because they care about the meaning of the work, not simply the mechanics of it. Trust is built on character, not capability. AI elevates capability; hidden talent protects character. That is the human edge.

Even the most advanced machine-learning systems operate on data that reflects what has already been. But hidden talent operates on an internal compass oriented towards what should be. They see not only the pattern but also the responsibility behind it. They do not simply execute tasks, they hold space for the ethical, emotional, and relational weight that accompanies decisions. When a crisis hits, leaders quickly realise that technology may be powerful, but it is human steadiness that prevents collapse. And it is often the quiet individuals, the overlooked experts, the ones who don't seek credit, who carry the organisation through its most vulnerable moments. This is not romanticism; it is a pattern observable across industries. Automated systems hold the ship steady; hidden talent ensures it stays on course.

There is another nuance worth naming: AI amplifies both strengths and weaknesses within an organisation. It makes your processes faster, but it also accelerates your dysfunctions. It makes your decisions more efficient, but it also magnifies errors at scale. When hidden talent is woven into the system, it acts as the natural counterbalance to this acceleration. They question assumptions before the system locks them in. They test hypotheses in ways no algorithm is trained to do. They sense misalignment before it becomes a structural fault. Their depth becomes a stabiliser, grounding the organisation in a form of care that artificial intelligence cannot replicate. AI can scale intelligence, but not integrity.

What we are witnessing is not a competition between humans and machines, it is the emergence of a partnership where hidden talent is more essential than ever. The organisations that will thrive are those that recognise this symbiosis early and refuse to treat talent as a disposable resource simply because technology appears more economical. Hidden talent brings a texture that is impossible to fabricate: the humility to admit what they don't know, the instinct to collaborate rather than dominate, the discipline to follow through, the maturity to navigate complexity without theatrics, the sense of stewardship that rises when people take genuine ownership of outcomes. These are qualities that algorithms cannot model.

And yet, for all their value, hidden talent still struggles in the shadows, particularly in an era where AI dazzles leaders with its speed, confidence, and sophistication. Too many organisations mistakenly equate automation with progress, forgetting that progress without ethics is simply acceleration. The urgency now is not to replace people with machines, but to redesign systems that amplify the quiet intelligence of hidden talent rather than overshadow it. Technology should serve their judgment, not substitute for it. AI should lighten their load, not silence their contributions. Digital transformation should increase their reach, not diminish their relevance.

The truth is that hidden talent embodies something profoundly future-proof: they are the keepers of nuance in a world obsessed with certainty. They are the final firewall against poor decisions. They are the moral centre of systems designed to optimise everything except meaning. As AI grows in capability, the spaces where human depth becomes sharper, not smaller. Complexity does not eliminate the need for humans; it elevates the need for humans who think deeply, act responsibly, and operate without ego. These are the people who ensure that technology remains a tool rather than a tyrant.

If there is one defining characteristic of hidden talent, it is their innate sense of ownership, the quiet, determined belief that if something is worth doing, it is worth doing well. AI can repeat tasks indefinitely, but it cannot care. It cannot feel accountable for the outcome. It cannot lie awake at night running through possible scenarios. It cannot choose integrity over convenience. It cannot wrestle with doubt to find clarity. Only humans can do that, only humans with depth, humility, and an internal code strong enough to resist pressure. Ownership is the human signature that AI cannot forge. Organisations that forget this will find themselves technologically advanced yet morally hollow.

The future belongs not to the loudest voices or the most cutting-edge tools, but to teams of depth, teams where technology amplifies the strengths of hidden talent rather than overshadowing them. The organisations that thrive will be those that recognise AI not as a replacement for human judgement, but as an ally to it. Leaders who understand this will design environments in which integrity is not negotiable, hidden talent is not invisible, character is recognised as a strategic asset, and the human edge becomes the defining advantage in a world driven by machines.

And as automation continues to rise, one truth becomes impossible to ignore: technology may change how we work, but hidden talent will determine why it matters. The future of organisational excellence lies not in algorithms alone, but in the quiet, unshakeable strength of the humans who stand behind them.

Retention and Career Pathing

Organisations have long struggled with retention. High turnover costs not only financial resources but also knowledge, relational capital, and momentum. Yet for hidden talent, those individuals who deliver quietly, consistently, and without fanfare, retention dynamics are particularly nuanced. They do not seek attention, promotions, or public accolades in the ways traditional talent might. They thrive on autonomy, meaningful work, purpose, and trust. To retain such individuals, organisations must rethink conventional approaches to career development, moving beyond linear progression, titles, or visibility-based recognition. Retention of hidden talent is not about forcing them into a mould; it is about understanding their intrinsic drivers, providing aligned growth opportunities, and creating an environment in which their unique capabilities are preserved, nurtured, and amplified.

At the heart of retention strategy lies psychological alignment. Hidden talent is driven by impact and mastery, not status or external recognition. They measure success internally: solving complex problems, stabilising operations, supporting colleagues, and contributing to outcomes that matter. For many, public recognition or promotion can even be counterproductive if it interferes with their preferred working style. Leaders who understand these internal motivators can craft retention strategies that are subtle yet powerful, focusing on aligning individual purpose with organisational objectives. Recognition, then, becomes strategic, reinforcing impact without forcing visibility, celebrating outcomes rather than performance theatre.

Retention begins with understanding individual preferences and strengths. Standard career paths often assume that everyone desires a trajectory of increasing visibility, management responsibility, or broader scope. For hidden talent, such assumptions are usually false. Many prefer roles where influence is exercised quietly, through decision-making, mentorship, problem-solving, or operational excellence. Career pathing for these individuals must therefore be flexible and multidimensional. It should enable vertical growth, lateral expansion, skill deepening, and cross-functional deployment without requiring public performance. This requires leaders to listen attentively, observe patterns of behaviour and contributions, and map growth opportunities in ways that respect personal working styles and cognitive preferences.

An effective retention strategy also incorporates autonomy and ownership. Hidden talent thrives in environments where they can exercise judgement, manage workflows, and take responsibility for outcomes without micromanagement. Delegating authority, providing clear expectations, and allowing discretion foster intrinsic motivation, which in turn drives engagement and loyalty. When individuals feel trusted to manage their domain, they are less likely to seek opportunities elsewhere. Retention is not simply about incentives; it is about cultivating a professional environment in which autonomy, competence, and purpose coexist.

Another critical component is strategic visibility without exposure. Hidden talent often operates behind the scenes, stabilising processes, mentoring peers, and anticipating risks. While they may not seek recognition, the organisation must remain aware of their contributions to prevent underappreciation. Leaders can create mechanisms that surface internal impact: executive briefings that highlight outcomes, team reflections on contributions, or inclusion in decision-making forums, without requiring public presentations. This reinforces the sense of purpose, ensures alignment with organisational objectives, and prevents the frustration that often drives attrition.

Mentorship and peer networks are also essential in retaining hidden talent. Many of these individuals are highly relational, providing guidance to colleagues and facilitating cross-team problem-solving. Formalising mentorship opportunities allows them to influence outcomes while maintaining the discretion they prefer. Peer networks offer support, knowledge exchange, and validation, which are critical for sustaining engagement. By embedding hidden talent into these relational structures, organisations create a sense of belonging and reinforce the value of their contributions without requiring performative visibility.

Career pathing for hidden talent must also account for skill development and capability growth. Stagnation is a standard driver of attrition. Even individuals who are content in their current roles seek opportunities to deepen expertise, explore adjacent domains, or take on challenges that stretch their problem-solving capacity. Organisations can design rotational projects, cross-functional assignments, or advanced skill development programmes tailored to these needs. By linking growth opportunities directly to individual strengths and interests, leaders create a pathway that preserves engagement while expanding capability, ensuring that hidden talent continues to deliver value and sees a sustainable future within the organisation.

Recognition of cognitive load and resilience is another pillar of retention. Hidden talent often assumes responsibility for stabilising processes, solving complex problems, and mitigating risks, which carries a high cognitive and emotional load. Without acknowledging this burden, even subtly, individuals may experience stress, fatigue, and eventual disengagement. Leaders should monitor workloads, provide support systems, and ensure responsibilities do not become overwhelming. This may include periodic check-ins, delegated support structures, or AI-assisted workflow management to reduce repetitive work. Recognising the invisible labour of hidden talent is not about public accolades; it is about protecting cognitive capacity and sustaining long-term engagement.

Organisations that retain hidden talent also prioritise values alignment and cultural fit. These individuals are often highly attuned to organisational integrity, ethical standards, and consistency between stated values and lived experience. Misalignment can trigger attrition more than financial incentives ever could. Leaders must ensure that organisational culture respects discretion, collaboration, and purpose-driven work. Policies, recognition frameworks, and decision-making structures should reinforce these values. Hidden talent thrives in environments that enable it to operate authentically, autonomously, and aligned with meaningful goals.

Structured career frameworks for hidden talent differ fundamentally from conventional models. Rather than linear ladders, the paths are lattice-like: multidirectional, flexible, and skills-focused. Vertical promotions may be available for those seeking visibility, but lateral moves, deepening expertise, or project-based leadership roles offer meaningful growth without compromising their working style. These paths must be transparent, accessible, and communicated in ways that respect preference and discretion. Leaders must actively co-create these paths with individuals, incorporating feedback, observing performance patterns, and adapting opportunities to changing business needs and personal growth trajectories.

Retention strategies also leverage impact-driven feedback mechanisms. Traditional performance reviews, focused on visibility, metrics, or social presence, are often misaligned with the values of hidden talent. Instead, feedback should emphasise contribution, problem-solving, relational influence, and outcomes achieved. Regular, precise, and constructive feedback sustains engagement, reinforces alignment, and signals that the organisation values impact over spectacle. Such mechanisms prevent the alienation that leads to attrition while ensuring continuous professional development.

Succession planning for hidden talent is another critical factor. While many of these individuals do not seek high-profile leadership roles, their expertise and influence are vital for organisational resilience. Succession planning should identify pathways that allow hidden talent to mentor, advise, or guide strategic initiatives while maintaining discretion. This not only preserves continuity of knowledge but also reinforces a sense of purpose and belonging. Organisations that fail to plan for succession risk losing both capability and stability, while those that embed hidden talent into long-term strategic planning secure enduring advantage.

A nuanced approach to compensation and incentives further supports retention. Financial rewards alone rarely motivate hidden talent; recognition of skill, influence, and contribution is more meaningful. Incentive structures should be aligned with outcomes and impact, rather than volume or visibility. Opportunities for professional development, advanced problem-solving projects, and influence over organisational priorities are often more compelling than standard promotions or bonuses. Organisations that combine tangible rewards with strategic alignment preserve loyalty while reinforcing intrinsic motivation.

Flexible working arrangements are a modern retention lever that aligns particularly well with hidden talent. These individuals often prioritise focus, deep work, and autonomy over visibility and traditional office presence. Hybrid schedules, project-based flexibility, or asynchronous collaboration empower them to deliver optimally while maintaining personal well-being. Flexibility does not equate to leniency; it is a tool to align work style with capability, ensuring sustainable engagement and mitigating the risk of burnout.

Equally important is career enrichment through strategic challenges. Hidden talent thrives when given opportunities to solve complex problems, navigate ambiguity, and influence outcomes without necessarily receiving recognition. Leaders can design projects that stretch capability, integrate cross-functional collaboration, or address critical organisational priorities. By aligning challenge with competence, organisations create professional growth that is both motivating and rewarding, reducing attrition and reinforcing long-term engagement.

Retention is ultimately a relational endeavour. Hidden talent is highly sensitive to trust, respect, and authenticity in leadership. They respond positively to leaders who understand their contribution, create environments that preserve autonomy, and demonstrate alignment between words and actions. A culture of reliability, fairness, and discretion fosters loyalty. Conversely, leaders who apply one-size-fits-all retention strategies, relying solely on visibility, hierarchy, or extrinsic rewards, risk disengagement and attrition. Retention of hidden talent is not transactional; it is relational, strategic, and deeply human.

Organisational systems play a supporting role. HR processes, performance management, and succession frameworks must be designed to capture the nuanced contributions of hidden talent. Standard metrics of visibility, presentation, or quantity are inadequate. Instead, organisations must develop assessment frameworks that account for influence, problem-solving, consistency, relational contribution, and foresight. By codifying recognition of subtle but critical performance, organisations reinforce retention through structural validation of value.

Finally, retention and career pathing intersect with organisational strategy. Hidden talent is not merely an operational resource; it is strategic capital. Their ability to stabilise processes, influence networks, and anticipate risks underpins organisational resilience and agility. Career frameworks must therefore integrate business priorities with individual growth. Leaders must co-create development pathways that balance organisational need with personal preference, ensuring that hidden talent remains both engaged and optimally deployed.

In practice, successful retention of hidden talent requires continuous attention and adaptation. It demands observation without intrusion, feedback without performative pressure, challenge without overwhelming, and recognition without spectacle. Leaders must embrace empathy, strategic foresight, and a deep understanding of human psychology. Organisations that master these principles cultivate not only loyalty but sustained high performance, resilience, and adaptability. Hidden talent becomes a stabilising force, an engine of innovation, and a multiplier of organisational capability.

Retention and career pathing, therefore, are not ancillary functions. They are strategic imperatives. By understanding the intrinsic drivers of hidden talent, creating flexible yet meaningful career pathways, leveraging autonomy and trust, embedding recognition and challenge into professional development, and aligning organisational structures with capability rather than visibility, leaders secure an enduring competitive advantage. Organisations that fail to do so risk losing their most reliable, stabilising, and strategically valuable individuals, the very people whose absence is felt only when it is too late.

The ultimate lesson is this: hidden talent does not conform to conventional career paths, nor does it thrive under traditional retention models. Its value lies in subtlety, reliability, foresight, and relational influence. To preserve it, organisations must act deliberately, designing systems, culture, and career pathways that respect preference, amplify capability, and align personal purpose with organisational strategy. When done effectively, retention is not merely about keeping individuals; it is about sustaining the invisible engine that drives enduring organisational success.

Retention and career pathing for hidden talent is, in essence, an art, combining human psychology, leadership insight, and organisational strategy into a coherent, deliberate practice. It requires patience, observation, and a commitment to valuing impact over visibility. For organisations willing to invest in this practice, the rewards are profound: lower attrition, stronger culture, higher resilience, and a workforce capable of delivering excellence quietly, consistently, and sustainably. Hidden talent, when understood and nurtured, becomes not only an asset but the very backbone of organisational continuity and growth, shaping the present while safeguarding the future.

The work of retaining hidden talent and designing thoughtful career pathways is not a one-time initiative. It is ongoing, adaptive, and evolutionary, requiring constant reflection, adjustment, and responsiveness to changing business needs, technological shifts, and human dynamics. Organisations that embed this mindset cultivate loyalty, elevate impact, and create a sustainable ecosystem where hidden talent continues to thrive, and in doing so, secure a foundation of success that is invisible, yet unmistakably powerful.

The Future of Smart Organisations

Imagine walking into an office in 2028. Not the static, cubicle-filled workplaces of old, but a dynamic ecosystem: people, AI-agents, digital dashboards and quiet nodes of human influence weaving together. Some desks sit empty part of the week, but tasks still get done, delivery milestones are met ahead of time, and crises are averted before they emerge. There is no frantic firefighting, no frantic post-mortems, just a steady hum of productivity, resilience, and innovation. At the heart of this hum are not necessarily the loudest voices, the biggest titles, or the most visible "stars." They are the quiet thinkers, the silent deliverers, the hidden talent, working in tandem with machines and structure to create a more innovative organisation.

This is not a distant fantasy. The trajectory we are on suggests this future is already unfolding. In recent years, organisations have begun embedding AI deeply into their workflows, not as a novelty, but as infrastructure. What changes in the subsequent few cycles aren't just about tools or automation. It's a systemic shift in how work is done, how talent is recognised, and how organisations leverage the hidden engines of human capability rather than relying solely on hierarchy, visibility, or traditional metrics. To navigate this transition, and to thrive, leaders must understand a new architecture: one in which human subtlety, relational intelligence, and invisible influence combine with machine speed, scale, and consistency.

Human-AI Teams: The New Normal

We are entering an era in which the traditional concept of "hybrid work", partly remote, partly on-site, evolves into something more profound: the hybrid workforce, a blend of humans and AI agents working side by side. (Forbes)

Studies show that combining human intuition with AI's pattern recognition, data synthesis, and routine execution significantly enhances productivity, not by replacing humans, but by augmenting our strengths. (SpringerLink) AI becomes a collaborator. Agents handle repetitive, predictable or administrative tasks. Machines sift through data, summarise trends, and draft routine documents. Meanwhile, humans focus on what machines cannot do: navigating ambiguity, exercising judgment, building trust, and connecting the dots across organisational boundaries, precisely the domain of hidden talent.

Significantly, this shift changes not only what we work on but also how we structure teams and define roles. Tasks once bundled under a single job description may now be redistributed: some to AI, some to human specialists, and some to hybrid micro-teams. For organisations, this unlocks tremendous flexibility and scalability. But it also opens the door to a deeper challenge, and opportunity: how to recognise and harness human talent that thrives not on visibility but on influence, discretion, and subtlety.

If AI becomes part of the workforce, success will depend not on AI alone, but on a new kind of human-machine alignment. One in which human relational intelligence, problem-solving, and tacit knowledge combine with AI's computational power to create collective intelligence, more innovative, faster, more creative. (SpringerLink)

Hidden Talent in the Age of Automation

When AI takes over repetitive tasks, scheduling, data analysis, routine correspondence, it reduces noise. It frees up human attention. It strips away the need to reward volume or visibility. That shift matters deeply for hidden talent. For generations, many quiet achievers have been overlooked, not because they lacked skill, but because their value was invisible or difficult to measure.

In an innovative organisation, those old biases become risks: the risk of neglecting what truly sustains performance. But they also present an opportunity to realign organisational values, systems, and incentives toward what truly matters. Outcome. Resilience. Stability. Innovation. When AI handles the routine, the spotlight no longer goes to noisy tasks, it goes where human judgement, subtlety, and trust still matter.

Research supports this shift. A 2024-25 literature review of generative AI in professional sectors noted that AI augments workflows across domains, but meaningful work remains rooted in human decision-making, collaboration, and creative problem-solving. (MDPI) When organisations treat AI as a collaboration tool rather than a replacement, they unlock a latent potential: human creativity and relational dynamics flourish. Hidden talent thrives because the spotlight shifts from visibility to value.

Moreover, studies of "human-AI collaboration" show that output quality is highest when humans remain deeply involved in shaping, guiding and supervising AI output, not when they approve or edit it. (arXiv) In other words: AI can handle parts of tasks; humans still need to steer the ship, and that steering requires precisely the kind of quiet, thoughtful, context-aware work hidden talent is good at.

In the coming years, organisations that succeed will be those that recognise this dynamic. They will not view AI as a threat to people. They will view it as the scaffolding that lifts human capability, enabling subtle, high-impact work to scale. And they will design systems that surface, support, and amplify hidden talent, rather than reward volume and visibility alone.

The New Architecture of Work: Blended, Not Just Hybrid

If hybrid workplaces combine remote and in-office work, the next wave, "blended workforces", will combine human roles, AI co-workers, freelance talent, and dynamic project-based teams, regardless of geography or traditional structure. (arXiv)

In this architecture:

- Some tasks are fully automated.
- AI human teams handle some.
- Some remain firmly human because they require creativity, empathy, judgment, relational nuance, or strategic thinking.

Under this model, formal org-charts lose meaning. What matters are networks, of relationships, trust, and tacit knowledge, and capabilities, not rank. Hidden talent becomes more visible not because they speak up, but because their role becomes critical to the system's function.

This shift also redefines leadership. Leaders are no longer simply decision-makers; they are orchestral conductors, ensuring that AI, people, and organisational purpose move in harmony. Authentic leadership requires humility, emotional intelligence, and a deep commitment to developing human talent, especially those whose strengths lie in discretion and subtlety.

Designing Smart Organisations Around People, Not Processes

For organisations to ride this wave, they must focus on five interlocking dimensions: human readiness, talent strategy, culture, learning & development, and workflow design. These dimensions, when combined, create what some firms call "Talent Advantage." (EY)

1. Human Readiness, Psychological Safety, Trust, and Culture
With AI acting as a collaborator, not a replacement, organisations need to reinforce trust: in the integrity of systems, in the fairness of decision-making, and in the value of human judgement. Hidden talent thrives in environments where discretion is respected, mistakes are treated as opportunities for learning, and relationships, rather than outputs, are valued.

2. Talent Strategy, Skills, Potential, and Hidden Influence
As work becomes more fluid, organisations must map not just roles but capabilities: who can think strategically, who navigates ambiguity, who connects people, and who stabilises processes

under stress. Hidden talent becomes a strategic asset when understood in this way, especially when aligned with business priorities, succession planning, and resilience strategies.

3. Learning & Development, Continuous Adaptation, Upskilling, and AI Fluency
As AI and automation rapidly shift job demands, continuous learning becomes essential. But for hidden talent, often busy delivering quietly behind the scenes, learning systems must respect their work style: flexible, contextual, and autonomy-supporting. Organisations should embed learning into workflows, encourage microlearning, and emphasise human-AI collaboration skills, emotional intelligence, creativity, and systems thinking.

4. Workflow Design, Fluid Teams, Human-AI Pods, Distributed Authority
Rigid org charts and static role definitions give way to fluid, purpose-driven pods: human-AI teams assembled for each project based on required capabilities rather than rank. Hidden achievers may lead or advise multiple pods, contribute across functions, and influence critical decisions, not because their title says so, but because their expertise and trustworthiness matter.

5. Reward and Recognition Systems, Value Over Visibility
In the innovative organisation of the future, rewards should shift from “who speaks up most” to “who ensures things get done, sustainably, reliably, and well.” This demands a rethinking of performance evaluation, feedback loops, recognition practices, promotions, and incentives. Hidden talent should be valued not for volume or voice, but for impact, consistency, relational influence, foresight, and dependability.

What This Means for Hidden Talent, And for Leaders

For individuals who have long operated quietly, this future offers a powerful redefinition of value. Your strength is no longer invisibility. It becomes an agency. Your calm, your foresight, your relational intelligence, these are not quiet weaknesses, but strategic advantages. The coming era demands precisely what you already offer.

For leaders, this future offers a challenge, and a promise. The challenge is to shift mindsets: to see talent not as rigidly defined jobs, but as distributed capability. The promise is this: by recognising, nurturing, and empowering hidden talent, organisations can build resilience, agility, and potential beyond what traditional structures allow.

But success is not automatic. It depends on intention. It depends on aligning incentives with value, designing workflows with empathy, embedding learning with flexibility, and blending human judgment with machine capacity. The organisations that get there first, those who treat human-plus-AI as a symbiotic system, not a threat, will define the winners of the next decade.

A Scenario: Smart Organisations 2030, What It Looks Like

Imagine a mid-sized global services firm in 2030. Its workforce comprises:

- Human specialists, domain experts, relational connectors, problem solvers.

- AI agents, handling data analysis, scheduling, routine documentation, first-level triage, and infrastructure monitoring.
- Human-AI pods, dynamic teams assembled for a client project, a crisis response, or a new initiative.

Employees no longer clock hours; they deliver outcomes. Teams convene asynchronously, globally, sometimes with humans collaborating across time zones while AI agents maintain continuity overnight. Physical offices remain, not for desks, but for collaboration hubs: brainstorming rooms, rapid-prototyping centres, human-to-human connection spaces.

Performance reviews no longer focus on who spoke most or made the biggest presentation, but on who reliably delivered value, who stabilised flow, who connected people, who preserved institutional memory, and who innovated quietly but effectively. Talent maps highlight not only skills but also influence, network centrality, problem-solving agility, resilience under pressure, and human-AI fluency. Leadership teams look less like pyramids and more like constellations of capability: shifting, adaptive, and connected.

In this firm, hidden talent isn't just discovered, it is foundational. They are the backbone of resilience, the engine of innovation, the custodians of continuity. AI amplifies their work; workflow design leverages their subtle influence. The firm thrives, not because of shine and spectacle, but because of seamless, sustained performance rooted in human insight and machine support.

Preparing Today, Laying the Foundations for Smart Organisations

You don't need to wait until 2030 to get started. The foundations of an innovative organisation can, and should, be laid today.

- Begin by mapping talent not only by role but also by capabilities, influence networks, tacit knowledge, and resilience under pressure.
- Evaluate workflows to identify repetitive, routine tasks that AI or automation could absorb, freeing human attention for strategic, relational, creative work.
- Build learning programmes around human-AI collaboration: prompt engineering, AI literacy, decision-making, ethics, relational skills, systems thinking.
- Design flexible, purpose-driven teams: human-AI pods, cross-functional groups, dynamic deployment based on business priorities.
- Reimagine recognition and reward systems: value impact, consistency, relational influence, and problem-solving over visibility or volume.
- Cultivate a culture of psychological safety, trust, humility, acknowledging that automation doesn't replace human judgment but amplifies it.
- Develop leadership that understands orchestration, not command, leadership that shapes context, enables talent, and maintains the human-AI handshake.

When organisations take these steps, they move beyond treating AI as a cost-saving tool or a novelty. They treat it as a structural lever, a means to redesign work around human strength, to elevate hidden talent, and to build innovative, resilient, future-ready organisations.

Risks and Ethical Challenges, What to Watch Out For

This future, powerful as it is, is not without pitfalls. Automation and AI bring risks: overreliance on machines, erosion of institutional memory, dilution of human relationships, loss of psychological safety, new forms of inequality and exclusion. (EY)

Hidden talent, especially those who value discretion, may be siloed, overburdened, or left unseen. AI may automate visibility, reducing human roles to oversight. Recognition systems may collapse into metrics and dashboards. The organisational culture may tilt toward speed, scale, and automation at the expense of empathy, depth, and human connection.

Leaders must guard against these risks. They need to ensure that AI augments human work, not replaces human meaning; that visibility remains balanced with privacy; that automation does not decouple responsibility; and that culture, with its relational ties, unspoken norms, and tacit knowledge, does not erode into cold efficiency.

Ethical governance, human-centred design, transparent AI policy, continuous learning, and intentional cultural practices will determine which organisations survive, and which thrive. The future belongs to those who recognise technology is a tool. People, their values, subtlety, creativity, trust, and hidden influence, remain the real differentiator.

The Vision: Smart Organisations, Human-Centered, Future-Ready

The future of innovative organisations is not glamorous. It doesn't look like glitzy offices, open-plan spaces, or flashy titles. It seems quite competent. Enduring reliability. Adaptive teams. Human-AI alignment. A workforce that doesn't burn out under noise and pressure, but thrives on purpose, alignment, and discreet excellence.

In this future, hidden talent doesn't have to seek the spotlight. The spotlight shifts itself, toward value, not volume; toward impact, not applause; toward substance, not spectacle.

If you are a leader reading this now, this is your invitation: to build beyond the visible org chart. To design systems where invisible hands steer success. To recognise and amplify the people who deliver quietly but consistently. To marry human insight with machine capability.

And if you are one of those hidden achievers, those quiet stabilisers, problem-solvers, relational connectors, this is your promise: the world is waking up to the fact that you are not anomalies. You are central. You are essential. In tomorrow's innovative organisations, you will be foundational.

The future is not just about AI or hybrid work. It's about creating organisations that are human-first, intelligence-rich, and purpose-driven. Organisations that thrive not because of noise, but because of connection; not because of titles, but because of trust; not because of visibility, but because of value.

That future is not far away. It begins now.

SECTION VII

EXECUTION AND LEGACY

Making it real

How Smart Organisations Are Really Built

Throughout this book, we have explored the quiet currents that underpin organisational success, the people who deliver without drama, solve problems before they surface, and sustain systems when the spotlight is elsewhere. We have examined the psychology of recognition, the traits of silent deliverers, the strategies for empowering without visibility, the creation of talent maps, the amplification of impact through team design, the future of innovative organisations, and the subtle art of retention and career pathing. This final chapter synthesises these lessons into a single, coherent framework, a blueprint for discovering, developing, and deploying hidden talent at scale.

The Hidden Talent Blueprint rests on four interdependent pillars: Discover, Design, Deploy, and Sustain. Each pillar integrates human insight, strategic foresight, and organisational design, offering a path from recognition to impact and to long-term organisational advantage.

Discover: Identifying Hidden Talent

The first step is recognising that hidden talent exists and understanding why it often remains invisible. These are individuals whose contributions are subtle, relational, or context-dependent. They are not typically the loudest in meetings, nor do they aggressively pursue recognition. Their value manifests in stability, foresight, problem-solving, influence networks, and the ability to navigate complexity. Discovering hidden talent requires deliberate observation and an analytical mindset.

Leaders must move beyond superficial metrics and assess impact over visibility. Questions to guide discovery include: Who consistently resolves issues before they escalate? Who maintains continuity during crises? Who connects people, ideas, and processes across silos? Who balances cognitive load while sustaining performance? Mapping these individuals is both an art and a science. It draws on performance data, project outcomes, peer feedback, and network analysis, but it also requires intuition, the leader's ability to see patterns of influence that are not immediately measurable.

Psychology plays a crucial role in discovery. Hidden talent is often self-regulating, motivated by purpose rather than reward, and attuned to relational and systemic dynamics. Understanding motivation, cognitive load, and stress responses enables leaders to identify who is contributing in depth, even when that contribution is invisible. Recognising these dynamics early prevents disengagement and ensures that high-value contributors are nurtured before attrition becomes a risk.

AI and analytics tools offer powerful augmentation for discovery. Pattern recognition, workflow monitoring, and organisational network analysis can highlight individuals whose work underpins team and organisational success. When combined with human judgment, these tools provide a comprehensive view of influence, capability, and potential. However, discovery is not solely a technological exercise. Empathy, context awareness, and relational intelligence remain critical for distinguishing true hidden talent from transient high performers.

Design: Structuring Roles, Teams, and Pathways

Once hidden talent is identified, the next step is thoughtful design, creating roles, workflows, and career pathways that align with strengths, preferences, and organisational objectives. Design encompasses multiple dimensions: role clarity, team structure, workflow optimisation, and career mapping. Each dimension must preserve autonomy while amplifying impact.

Role design involves tailoring responsibilities to leverage cognitive strengths, relational skills, and problem-solving capabilities. Hidden talent thrives when given discretion, ownership, and a clear purpose. Over-structuring roles or imposing rigid hierarchies undermines engagement, while ambiguity without guidance creates stress. The goal is to strike a balance: sufficient clarity to align with organisational priorities, yet enough flexibility to enable innovation and discretion.

Team design is equally critical. Hidden talent often multiplies impact through relational influence, mentorship, and the stabilisation of complex processes. Teams should be structured to leverage these qualities by pairing quiet achievers with complementary skills, integrating AI and automation to handle routine work, and creating pods that enable dynamic collaboration across functions. Hybrid teams, blending in-office, remote, and AI-augmented cooperation, facilitate the strategic deployment of hidden talent while maintaining continuity and scalability.

Career pathing must depart from traditional linear models. Hidden talent often prefers lateral moves, deepening expertise, or project-based influence rather than climbing hierarchical ladders. Career frameworks should be flexible, multi-dimensional, and aligned with individual motivation and organisational needs. Rotational projects, cross-functional assignments, and skill-development initiatives sustain engagement and prevent stagnation, while recognising contributions in ways that respect discretion and intrinsic motivation.

Design also includes recognition systems. Traditional performance metrics often overlook subtle contributions. Instead, organisations should develop frameworks that capture relational influence, problem-solving, foresight, and resilience. Feedback should be specific, constructive, and delivered in ways that reinforce impact without forcing visibility. Recognition is most effective when it validates contributions, respects work styles and balances extrinsic reinforcement with intrinsic motivation.

Deploy: Amplifying Impact

The deployment of hidden talent is where strategy translates into measurable organisational advantage. Deployment is not merely assigning tasks; it is about aligning capability with priority, influence with decision-making, and discretion with autonomy. This requires careful orchestration of work, workflows, and networks.

One core principle is strategic delegation. Hidden talent often delivers disproportionately when entrusted with meaningful responsibility and the authority to execute. Leaders must delegate in ways that preserve autonomy while ensuring alignment with organisational objectives. This includes defining clear outcomes, providing necessary resources, and avoiding micromanagement, thereby converting potential into sustained impact.

Another principle is network amplification. Hidden talent exerts influence not only through formal authority but through relational and knowledge networks. Deployment strategies should map these networks and leverage them to amplify impact across teams, projects, and functions. Identifying key nodes of influence enables leaders to position hidden talent to stabilise processes, resolve bottlenecks, and guide decision-making without overt visibility.

Integration with AI and hybrid workflows further enhances deployment. Machines can handle routine, predictable, or data-intensive tasks, freeing hidden talent to focus on higher-order problem-solving, strategy, and relational coordination. AI can also support decision-making, surface insights, and maintain continuity across time zones and distributed teams. Aligning human judgment with machine augmentation enables hidden talent to operate at maximum effectiveness, thereby extending their reach and impact.

Deployment is also about managing cognitive load and resilience. Hidden talent is frequently responsible for stabilising systems, mentoring colleagues, and anticipating risks. Leaders must ensure that workloads are sustainable, that support structures are in place, and that recognition is aligned with contribution. Strategic use of technology, collaborative design, and periodic review can prevent burnout and sustain long-term performance.

Sustain: Retention, Growth, and Organisational Alignment

Sustainability is the final pillar of the blueprint, ensuring that hidden talent remains engaged, motivated, and aligned over time. Retention requires understanding intrinsic motivators, providing meaningful challenge, and creating environments where impact is recognised without forcing visibility. Career paths must be flexible, growth-oriented, and aligned with personal preference.

Psychological safety is central to sustainability. Hidden talent thrives where mistakes are treated as learning opportunities, autonomy is respected, and relational trust is maintained. Organisations must foster cultures that value discretion, reliability, and contribution over performance theatre. Leaders must model behaviour that respects working style, encourages collaboration, and validates subtle influence.

Sustainability also requires ongoing talent mapping and capability development. As organisational priorities evolve, so too must deployment and growth opportunities. Hidden talent should be continuously assessed for emerging skills, potential for cross-functional influence, and alignment with strategic objectives. Learning initiatives, mentorship, and exposure to new challenges ensure that engagement remains high and capability grows in tandem with organisational needs.

Recognition systems must evolve alongside work. Metrics that capture impact, relational influence, foresight, and resilience provide a holistic view of contribution. Feedback should be regular, meaningful, and tied to tangible outcomes. Reward mechanisms should integrate financial incentives, professional development, and influence-based recognition to maintain alignment with intrinsic motivation.

Finally, sustaining hidden talent requires integration with organisational strategy. These individuals are not peripheral resources; they are central to resilience, innovation, and continuity. Organisations that embed hidden talent into planning, decision-making, and knowledge continuity gain a strategic advantage that extends beyond individual performance. Succession planning, knowledge transfer, and leadership pipelines must account for these individuals' unique contributions to ensure their impact endures and grows over time.

The Integrated Blueprint

The Hidden Talent Blueprint, Discover, Design, Deploy, Sustain, is a dynamic, interconnected framework. Discovery identifies those whose impact is invisible but critical. Design creates conditions, pathways, and workflows that leverage strengths while respecting preferences. Deployment aligns capabilities with priorities, amplifying influence through strategic positioning, team structures, and technology integration. Sustain ensures long-term engagement, growth, and alignment with organisational objectives. Together, these pillars form a continuous loop: discovery informs design, design enables deployment, deployment reinforces retention, and sustainability guides further discovery and evolution.

In practice, organisations that adopt this blueprint experience multiple advantages: reduced attrition, higher engagement, increased productivity, and more resilient systems. Hidden talent is no longer overlooked or underutilised; it becomes the backbone of strategy, innovation, and operational excellence. AI and hybrid teams magnify this effect, not replacing human judgment but extending reach, enabling deeper focus, and enhancing collective intelligence.

Leaders who apply this blueprint gain a competitive edge by recognising the invisible engine of their organisation and structuring systems to multiply its impact. They learn to measure influence rather than noise, contribution rather than visibility, and stability rather than spectacle. By co-creating flexible career paths, embedding hidden talent into strategic initiatives, and designing cultures that preserve autonomy while recognising impact, they unlock potential that traditional approaches cannot reach.

The blueprint also reframes leadership itself. Success is no longer about commanding attention, managing visibility, or rewarding volume. It is about orchestration: aligning human and technological capability, fostering psychological safety, amplifying influence, and guiding the organisation toward outcomes that matter. Leaders become enablers of impact rather than gatekeepers of attention, custodians of capability rather than arbiters of recognition.

The final insight of this book is simple yet profound: hidden talent is the invisible engine of organisational success. Its retention, development, and amplification require deliberate strategy, empathy, and foresight. Organisations that map, deploy, and nurture these individuals gain resilience, innovation, and sustained competitive advantage. Those who overlook them risk attrition, inefficiency, and the erosion of institutional knowledge.

By following the Hidden Talent Blueprint, discovering capability, designing roles and pathways, deploying influence strategically, and sustaining engagement, leaders create organisations that are human-first, intelligence-rich, and future-ready. They build systems in which quiet excellence drives outcomes, subtle influence shapes decisions, and hidden talent is recognised not for spectacle but for enduring impact.

Ultimately, success in the modern organisation is not measured by visibility, applause, or volume. It is measured by continuity, foresight, resilience, and the quiet, sustained delivery of those who work without fanfare. Hidden talent is not peripheral; it is central. And the organisations that unlock its potential are the ones that will thrive, quietly, profoundly, and enduringly, in the decades to come.

The Hidden Talent Blueprint: Practical Implementation Guide

Imagine a circular flow diagram with four interconnected pillars: Discover → Design → Deploy → Sustain. Arrows move clockwise, representing continuous iteration, with feedback loops connecting Sustain back to Discover. Each pillar has key action points.

Step-by-Step Implementation

1. Discover: Identify Hidden Talent

Objective: Recognise individuals whose impact is high, but visibility is low.

Actions:

- Conduct organisational network analysis to map influence beyond formal hierarchy.
- Observe problem-solving patterns: who anticipates issues and resolves them quietly?
- Gather peer and manager feedback focused on relational impact, reliability, and foresight.
- Use psychological insights: assess motivation, cognitive strengths, resilience, and stress responses.

- Integrate AI-assisted analytics: workflow patterns, project completion data, and knowledge network mapping.

Key Outcome: A living map of hidden talent highlighting influence, skills, and relational networks.

2. Design: Structure Roles, Teams, and Career Paths

Objective: Align organisational structures and growth opportunities with individual strengths and preferences.

Actions:

- Tailor roles to leverage skills and cognitive strengths; provide autonomy and decision-making authority.
- Design teams with complementary skills, integrating hidden talent into critical functions and cross-functional projects.
- Develop flexible career paths: lateral moves, rotational projects, skill deepening, and project-based leadership roles.
- Implement recognition frameworks that validate contribution without forcing visibility.
- Embed AI tools to handle routine tasks, freeing hidden talent for high-value work.

Key Outcome: Roles, workflows, and career paths that amplify hidden talent without compromising autonomy.

3. Deploy: Amplify Impact

Objective: Position hidden talent strategically to maximise organisational influence.

Actions:

- Strategic delegation: assign responsibilities that match skills and provide autonomy.
- Leverage relational networks: place individuals where influence stabilises processes and drives decisions.
- Align with organisational priorities: deploy talent where impact is maximised, not where visibility is sought.
- Monitor cognitive load and stress to ensure sustained engagement through support structures and AI-assisted workflow management.
- Integrate AI and hybrid workflows to enable focus on higher-order problem-solving, creativity, and strategic judgment.

Key Outcome: Hidden talent is actively shaping outcomes, stabilising processes, and multiplying organisational capability.

4. Sustain: Retain, Develop, and Align

Objective: Ensure long-term engagement, growth, and alignment with organisational strategy.

Actions:

- Psychological safety: maintain trust, autonomy, and relational support.

- Flexible career pathways: provide meaningful challenge, skill evolution, and cross-functional exposure.
- Continuous feedback: emphasise contribution, foresight, relational influence, and problem-solving impact.
- Succession planning: embed hidden talent into knowledge continuity and strategic initiatives.
- Values alignment: maintain a culture that respects discretion, collaboration, and purpose-driven work.
- Incentives aligned with impact: combine financial, developmental, and influence-based recognition.

Key Outcome: Hidden talent remains engaged, valued, and integrated into the long-term strategy of the organisation.

Iteration and Continuous Improvement

- Feedback Loops: Use insights from Sustain to inform Discover. Hidden talent evolves; so, should identification methods.
- Adjust Design: Roles, workflows, and career paths should adapt to changing business needs and individual development.
- Refine Deployment: Reallocate talent strategically in response to evolving organisational priorities, networks, and technology integration.
- Evaluate Retention Strategies: Continuously assess engagement, satisfaction, and motivation metrics to prevent attrition.

Implementation Checklist

1. Map influence and hidden talent across the organisation.
2. Tailor roles and teams to amplify impact while respecting autonomy.
3. Deploy talent strategically in line with organisational priorities.
4. Integrate AI and technology as enablers rather than replacements.
5. Create flexible, meaningful career pathways.
6. Maintain psychological safety and values alignment.
7. Implement recognition and reward systems focused on impact.
8. Monitor engagement, workload, and cognitive health.
9. Embed succession planning and knowledge continuity.
10. Iterate continuously based on feedback from performance, network, and engagement data.

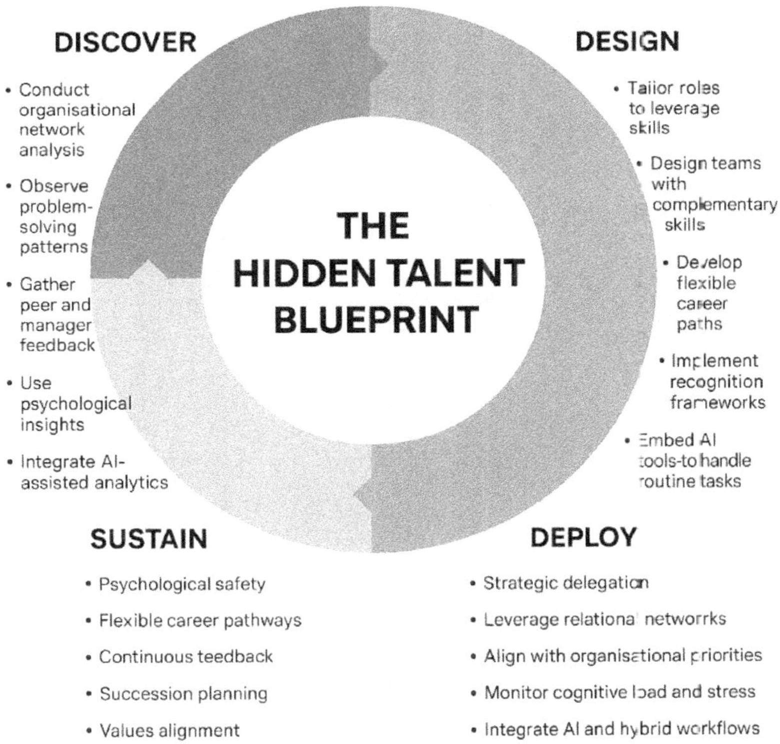
THE
HIDDEN TALENT
BLUEPRINT
DISCOVER
• Conduct organisational network analysis
• Observe problem-solving patterns
• Gather peer and manager feedback
• Use psychological insights
• Integrate AI-assisted analytics
DESIGN
• Tailor roles to leverage skills
• Design teams with complementary skills
• Develop flexible career paths
• Implement recognition frameworks
• Embed AI tools-to handle routine tasks
SUSTAIN
• Psychological safety
• Flexible career pathways
• Continuous teedback
• Succession planning
• Values alignment
DEPLOY
• Strategic delegation
• Leverage relational networrks
• Align with organisational priorities
• Monitor cognitive load and stress
• Integrate AI and hybrid workflows

CLOSING

What Changes When You Truly See

There is a moment that arrives quietly for every leader who learns to see appropriately. It is not dramatic. There is no announcement. No shift in title or authority. What changes is something more fundamental. The way the organisation appears to you has changed.

Until now, leadership has often felt like navigating by signals. Dashboards, updates, meetings, summaries. You learn to interpret the organisation through what reaches you. After this moment, leadership becomes something else entirely. You begin to sense what is happening even when no one is speaking.

This is not intuition in the mystical sense. It is perception, trained and recalibrated.

When you truly see, you stop confusing activity with progress. Noise no longer reassures you. Silence no longer alarms you. You begin to distinguish between motion and movement. You notice who creates stability rather than attention. You recognise the difference between people who manage risk and people who absorb it.

This shift changes how you listen.

You stop rewarding fluency as a proxy for understanding. You stop assuming that confidence equals competence. You grow comfortable with pauses, with partial answers, with thoughtful uncertainty. You give space to those who think before they speak, and you realise how much you were missing when you did not.

Seeing properly also changes how you decide.

Decisions become less performative. You feel less pressure to be visibly decisive and more responsibility to be quietly correct. You consult differently. You seek counsel from those closest to the work rather than those closest to you. You ask fewer questions about status and more about strain.

You begin to understand that an organisation's health is not revealed in moments of success but in how it behaves under pressure. Who steps forward without being asked? Who simplifies complexity for others. Who protects the system even when no one is watching?

When you truly see, your relationship with power changes.

You use it more sparingly. You recognise that authority is loud, but influence is subtle. You stop pulling every decision upward and allow competence to operate where it lives. You trust judgment rather than controlling outcomes. This does not weaken leadership. It strengthens it.

Something else changes, too. The organisation begins to change in response.

Hidden talent does not require motivation. It needs to be recognised in its own language. When people feel seen without being exposed, something unlocks. They contribute more, not because they are asked, but because the environment finally feels safe for contribution. Ideas surface earlier. Risks are raised sooner. Problems are solved before they become visible.

The organisation becomes calmer.

Not slower. Calmer.

There are fewer unnecessary escalations. Fewer performative meetings. Less energy spent managing perception. More energy spent doing work that matters. Leaders often describe this as increased maturity, but what they are really experiencing is the return of trust.

Seeing properly also changes how you measure success.

You stop overvaluing what can be easily counted and start paying attention to what can only be sensed. Reliability. Judgement. Stewardship. You understand that some of the most valuable work in your organisation will never be fully visible, and that this is not a flaw but a feature.

This way of seeing makes you patient.

You no longer expect immediate proof of impact from every change. You understand that cultures shift quietly before they shift visibly. You are less reactive and more observant. Less performative and more deliberate.

Perhaps the most profound change is internal.

Leadership feels lighter.

Not because responsibility has diminished, but because you are no longer carrying it alone. When hidden talent is recognised and trusted, leadership becomes distributed. The organisation ceases to rely on heroic intervention and instead relies on collective competence.

This is not a new management philosophy. It is an old truth that modern organisations have forgotten.

Strong systems are built by people who care deeply and speak softly. Enduring performance is created by those who take ownership without applause. Stability comes from individuals who see their role not as advancing themselves, but as protecting the whole.

When you truly see, you begin to design organisations around these realities rather than against them.

You build structures that reward substance over spectacle. You create pathways that do not require self-promotion to progress. You recognise that the future will belong not to the loudest voices, but to the clearest thinkers.

This way of seeing does not make leadership easier. It makes it truer.

And once you have learned to see in this way, you cannot unsee it.

You will notice the quiet contributors in every room. You will sense when something is being held together by unseen effort. You will recognise an organisation as resilient not because it looks impressive, but because it feels steady.

This is the change that matters.

Not a new framework.
Not a new process.
Not a new title.

A new way of seeing.

And from that, everything else follows.

The Quiet Architecture of Enduring Organisations

There is a difference between organisations that impress and organisations that endure. The former are often loud, fast, and confident. They announce progress constantly. They celebrate activity. They perform competently in public. The latter are calmer. Less theatrical. More difficult to summarise in a slide deck. They do not look dramatic when things are going well, and they do not collapse under pressure. Their strength is structural, not performative.

This chapter is about that structure. Not the org chart. Not the strategy document. The quiet architecture beneath the surface determines whether an organisation bends or breaks when conditions change.

Most leaders believe endurance is a function of resilience plans, contingency funding, or crisis playbooks. Those matters are secondary. Endurance is built long before a crisis appears. It is built in how work is actually done, how judgment is distributed, how effort is recognised, and how silence is interpreted.

At the centre of this architecture sits hidden talent.

Heroics do not power enduring organisations. They are powered by reliability. By people who notice before others notice. By individuals who absorb friction without being asked. By teams that quietly stabilise outcomes while attention shifts elsewhere. These organisations do not depend on last-minute saves or dramatic interventions because they have already invested in the conditions that prevent collapse.

This investment is rarely deliberate. It is cultural. It accumulates through thousands of small choices. Who is listened to in meetings? Who is trusted with ambiguity? Who is protected from unnecessary noise? Who is promoted, and why? Over time, these choices harden into structure.

In fragile organisations, structure rewards visibility. In enduring organisations, structure rewards judgment.

Judgement is more complex to see than confidence. It does not announce itself. It shows up as fewer problems rather than more explanations. It produces calm rather than excitement. Leaders who have not learned to value this mistake fall into complacency. They assume that if nothing dramatic is happening, nothing important is happening.

The opposite is often true.

Quiet architecture is revealed in how organisations behave when nothing is broken, when deadlines are being met. When clients are satisfied. When systems appear stable, hidden talent does its most important work. It maintains equilibrium. It corrects minor deviations. It keeps complexity within tolerable bounds.

Because this work leaves no trace, it is easy to overlook. Leaders attribute success to strategy, culture, or market conditions. They rarely attribute it to the individuals who quietly ensured that decisions were made correctly, handovers were clean, and risks were intercepted early.

Enduring organisations do not make this mistake for long.

They learn, often through experience, that success without understanding is dangerous. That outcomes delivered without insight into how they were delivered create dependency without awareness. And dependency without awareness is fragility in disguise.

This is why so many organisations appear strong until they are tested. They have mistaken performance for capacity. They have optimised for presentation rather than foundation.

Quiet architecture is not accidental. It is the result of leaders choosing to value certain behaviours even when they are inconvenient to recognise. It means elevating those who prevent problems rather than those who explain them. It means designing roles that allow deep work rather than constant exposure. It means trusting people to act without asking for permission every time.

It also means accepting that some of the most valuable contributors will never fit the traditional image of leadership. They will not dominate rooms. They will not campaign for advancement. They will not always communicate in headlines. Their value emerges through consistency, foresight, and care.

Enduring organisations build around this reality rather than trying to change it.

They distribute authority closer to the work. They allow decisions to be made where information is richest. They resist pulling everything upward in the name of control. They understand that centralising decision-making often increases noise while reducing quality.

This does not mean a lack of leadership. It means a different expression of the same concept. Leaders in enduring organisations spend less time performing certainty and more time cultivating conditions. They are comfortable with not being the most intelligent person in the room. They ask questions that surface substance rather than speed. They create space for those who need time to think.

This is harder than it sounds.

Modern leadership culture rewards immediacy—quick answers. Clear narratives. Strong opinions delivered confidently. Quiet architecture asks leaders to tolerate ambiguity without prematurely filling it. To sit with partial information while judgment forms. To listen to those who speak carefully rather than those who speak often.

There is also an ethical dimension to this architecture. Enduring organisations recognise that it is unjust to extract value invisibly and reward it visibly elsewhere. They understand that fairness is not only a moral concern but a structural one. Systems that consistently reward noise over substance eventually drive away the very people who keep them functional.

Retention, in this sense, is not a benefit issue. It is a design issue.

When organisations are designed to see and protect hidden talent, loyalty follows naturally. People stay because their way of working is respected. Because they are not forced to become something they are not, they are not to be valued. Because they are trusted to carry responsibility without constant monitoring.

Trust is the load-bearing beam of quiet architecture.

Without it, organisations rely on control. Control generates reporting. Reporting generates noise. Noise obscures reality. Reality then surprises leadership. The cycle repeats.

With trust, organisations rely on judgement. Judgment reduces unnecessary oversight. Reduced oversight creates space for deep work. Deep work improves outcomes. Outcomes reinforce trust.

This is how endurance compounds.

There is a misconception that calm organisations lack ambition. In practice, the opposite is often true. Calm is not the absence of urgency. It is the presence of capability. When people know what they are doing and are allowed to do it, the organisation moves faster with less friction.

Urgency without capability creates drama. Capability without drama creates progress.

Another feature of quiet architecture is memory. Enduring organisations remember what almost went wrong, not just what went right. They learn from near misses. They value those who raise concerns early. They do not punish the messenger for being careful. They recognise that the absence of failure often results from paying attention.

This creates a culture where risk is managed intelligently rather than theatrically, where escalation is used sparingly, and where people are encouraged to resolve issues at the lowest sensible level rather than pushing everything upward for visibility.

In fragile organisations, people escalate to protect themselves. In enduring organisations, people resolve to protect the system.

The difference lies in how leaders respond when something small is raised. If leaders overreact, people learn to stay quiet. If leaders listen thoughtfully, people learn to speak early. Quiet architecture depends on this dynamic.

Technology complicates this further. Modern tools amplify noise effortlessly. Updates are cheap. Messages are constant. Visibility is continuous. In this environment, it takes deliberate effort to protect depth.

Enduring organisations do this by being selective. They reduce unnecessary communication. They protect time for thinking. They design rhythms of work that favour resolution over reporting. They do not confuse connectivity with collaboration.

They also understand that not all contribution should be broadcast. Some work is better left unannounced. Some problems are best solved quietly. Some success is more valuable when it does not attract attention.

This runs counter to much contemporary management advice, which equates transparency with constant sharing. Enduring organisations practice a more mature transparency. They share what matters, when it matters, with those who need it. They do not confuse openness with noise.

The architecture also extends to how organisations respond to success. In noisy cultures, success triggers celebration of individuals who were most visible. In enduring cultures, success triggers reflection on what allowed it to happen. Who supported it. What conditions enabled it. How those conditions can be preserved.

This subtle difference shapes incentives. People learn that value is recognised even when it is not shouted about. Over time, this attracts and retains a different kind of contributor. People who care about outcomes more than optics. People who prefer depth to display.

Such organisations are often described as having strong culture, but culture is an effect, not a cause. The cause is architecture. The decisions that determine what is rewarded, what is protected, and what is ignored.

Leaders who want to build enduring organisations must therefore become architects rather than performers. They must pay attention to load paths. Where pressure travels. Where it accumulates. Where it is absorbed. They must notice who is carrying weight silently and ask whether that is fair or sustainable.

This requires humility. It requires leaders to accept that their view is partial. That the organisation they experience is filtered through layers of narrative and noise. That some of the most important work happens out of sight.

The reward for this humility is profound. Leaders gain access to deeper insight. They are surprised less often. They make better decisions because those decisions are informed by people who understand the system intimately.

Over time, leadership itself becomes quieter. Less reactive. Less performative. More grounded.

This is often misinterpreted by outsiders. Enduring organisations are not flashy. They do not always dominate headlines. They do not constantly reinvent themselves. They focus on getting the basics right, consistently, and on protecting the people who make that possible.

When crisis arrives, as it always does eventually, the difference becomes visible. Fragile organisations scramble. Enduring organisations respond. Not because they have better plans, but because they have better judgement distributed throughout the system.

The quiet ones step forward, as they always have. The difference is that this time, they are not alone. The organisation has been designed to support them.

This is the quiet architecture of endurance.

It is not built through slogans or initiatives. It is built through attention. Through leaders choosing to notice what is usually ignored. Through reward systems that value impact over impression. Through trust extended thoughtfully rather than withheld reflexively.

Hidden talent is not an add on to this architecture. It is the foundation.

Organisations that understand this do not talk endlessly about resilience. They embody it. They do not chase noise. They cultivate value. They do not rely on heroics. They build reliability.

And when they succeed, it does not look dramatic. It looks steady. Calm. Unremarkable.

Until you compare it to what happens when that architecture is absent.

Then the difference is unmistakable.

Endurance, it turns out, is quiet work done well, by people who do not need the spotlight, in organisations wise enough to see them.

Epilogue: Unlocking the Invisible Engine

For decades, organisations have chased the visible markers of success: titles, presentations, awards, and quarterly metrics. Leaders have been taught to measure performance by presence, volume, and easily quantifiable output. Yet beneath every successful operation, every innovation that changes the trajectory of a business, and every crisis that never became catastrophic, there exists another reality, the silent engine of achievement. This hidden talent quietly advances the organisation. These are the people who do not demand recognition or seek the spotlight, yet whose contributions underpin sustained success.

By now, you have walked through the layers of discovery, psychology, and strategy that make hidden talent visible in its impact, if not in their presence. You have explored the quiet deliverers who stabilise systems. These psychological principles shape motivation and resilience; the leadership approaches that empower without forcing visibility; the talent maps that translate subtle capabilities into strategic insight; and the ways in which teams can be structured to multiply impact. Finally, you have looked into the future, a world where AI, hybrid teams, and more innovative workplace practices intersect to amplify human potential.

But this epilogue is not merely a summary. It is a call to action, a reflection, and an invitation. The insights you have gained are meaningless without application. Hidden talent is not a theoretical construct; it is a living, breathing resource that requires deliberate, thoughtful stewardship. It is an asset that will not flourish under old paradigms of management, metrics, or visibility. It thrives under leaders who understand subtlety, who value influence over presence, and who design organisations to unlock latent potential.

The first truth is this: hidden talent thrives where it is trusted, not watched. Traditional management often conflates oversight with effectiveness. Managers check boxes, track hours, and measure deliverables, believing that visibility equals value. Hidden achievers operate differently. Their impact is relational, cognitive, and systemic. They prevent crises before they appear, connect dots that others cannot see, and stabilise complex processes without fanfare. Attempting to control, monitor excessively, or demand performative visibility does not increase impact; it diminishes it. Leaders must create space, trust judgment, and measure results, not activity.

Second, impact is multiplied, not broadcast. Throughout the chapters, we explored how team design, delegation, and knowledge networks enable hidden talent to scale influence without seeking recognition. This is the essence of amplification: creating conditions where subtle contributions propagate through an organisation, enhancing collective capability. Hidden talent does not require micro-management, but it does require structural support. Delegation must be intentional, workflow design must be adaptive, and relational networks must be recognised. When organisations understand this, they transform individual excellence into systemic advantage.

Third, psychology is the undercurrent of effectiveness. Cognitive load, stress response, motivation, and resilience shape every decision, every problem solved, and every crisis avoided. Hidden achievers often manage these dynamics intuitively: pacing themselves, regulating emotion, anticipating consequences, and balancing priorities. Leaders who seek to empower hidden talent must understand these psychological factors. Systems, expectations, and rewards must support cognitive bandwidth, reinforce intrinsic motivation, and reduce unnecessary friction. When organisations fail to account for psychology, they risk burnout, disengagement, and the loss of critical capability.

Fourth, talent mapping is a form of strategic foresight. Mapping hidden talent is not about creating org charts or filling spreadsheets with skills. It is about understanding who holds knowledge, who influences outcomes, and who can act decisively when others falter. It is about aligning individual capabilities with organisational priorities in a way that preserves autonomy while enhancing effectiveness. Leaders who master talent mapping can anticipate gaps, deploy resources strategically, and preserve institutional knowledge, all while keeping hidden talent engaged, motivated, and impactful.

Fifth, technology is an amplifier, not a replacement. As we have explored, AI and hybrid teams are reshaping the work landscape. Machines can process data faster, detect anomalies earlier, and perform repetitive tasks without fatigue. But machines cannot replicate judgment, relational influence, creativity, or ethical discernment. Hidden talent thrives in this new world because its unique human skills, subtle, relational, and adaptive, are amplified by technology. Organisations that integrate AI thoughtfully, treating it as a collaborator rather than a competitor, unlock hidden potential and multiply impact exponentially.

The vision of an innovative, flexible, resilient, human-centred, and intelligence-rich organisation is not futuristic. It begins with recognising what is already present: the people quietly driving success. They are stabilisers in crises, innovators in obscurity, connectors across networks, translators of complexity into action. They are the custodians of organisational memory, the unseen architects of workflows, and the interpreters of nuance that machines cannot grasp. By acknowledging, mapping, and empowering them, leaders transform invisible energy into measurable, sustained advantage.

Yet transformation requires courage. It is easier to reward visibility, to celebrate those who speak loudly, to prioritise metrics over subtle influence. But organisations that cling to old paradigms will miss the silent currents that sustain performance. They will invest in the wrong metrics, promote poor performers, and lose the very talent that ensures stability, agility, and innovation. Hidden talent does not flourish under short-termism, politics, or spectacle. It thrives under leaders who see beyond the obvious, who value contribution over applause, and who design systems that respect discretion, cognitive diversity, and relational intelligence.

To operationalise these lessons, leaders must take deliberate action. Begin by observing quietly: who solves problems before they arise? Who holds networks together? Who can be relied upon to deliver consistently, without fanfare? Document this insight in structured talent maps that capture capability, potential, relational influence, and motivation. Align these insights with strategic objectives to ensure deployment is purposeful, effective, and sustainable.

Next, structure teams for amplification, not visibility. Delegate authority thoughtfully, design workflows to leverage complementary strengths, and embed knowledge transfer mechanisms that allow hidden talent to scale influence: reward impact, consistency, and foresight rather than visibility or volume. Create psychological safety, trust, and autonomy as default conditions, not luxuries.

Third, embrace technology with humility and strategy. Identify tasks that AI or automation can handle efficiently, freeing human attention for complex judgment, relational dynamics, and creative problem-solving. Embed AI as a partner, not a replacement, and measure success in terms of amplified human impact, not merely efficiency gains.

Finally, cultivate a culture of recognition without spotlight. Hidden talent needs to feel valued without being forced into visibility. Recognition should reinforce alignment with outcomes, respect working styles, and preserve intrinsic motivation. When this balance is struck, motivation, retention, and organisational resilience soar.

The organisations of the future, those that thrive beyond 2026, will share a common characteristic: they understand that human capability extends beyond what can be seen in presentations, meetings, or dashboards. They recognise that impact is often invisible, influence is subtle, and contribution is relational. They design systems, teams, workflows, and technologies that amplify hidden talent rather than forcing it into performative roles. They balance autonomy with alignment, discretion with accountability, and psychology with strategy.

This is the ultimate lesson of Find the Hidden Talent: sustainable success is not created by the loudest, the most visible, or the most self-promoting. It is made by the quiet achievers, the relational stabilisers, the problem-solvers, and the strategic thinkers whose work is felt rather than seen. It is amplified by deliberate leadership, thoughtful structure, and intelligent use of technology. It is nurtured in cultures of trust, psychological safety, and respect for autonomy. It is preserved, scaled, and replicated through systematic mapping, deployment, and recognition.

If you are a leader, this is your opportunity: to see the unseen, value the undervalued, and structure the organisation around what truly drives impact. If you are a hidden achiever, this is your promise: your skills, your foresight, and your quiet influence are essential, central, and irreplaceable.

The future of work will not be about spectacle. It will be about substance. Titles will not define it; it is characterised by trust. It will not reward noise; it rewards outcomes. And at the centre of this future, quietly but powerfully, is hidden talent, the invisible engine that propels organisations toward resilience, agility, and enduring success.

The question is not whether your organisation recognises it. The question is whether you will act to amplify it.

Because the future belongs to those who do.

About The Author:

Mark Powell has spent 38 years navigating the complex terrain of global corporate leadership. A former Director at Standard Chartered Bank, he has built a reputation for creating superpower teams that deliver extraordinary results in high-pressure, high-stakes environments.

Mark combines his deep expertise in psychology with a pragmatic approach to organisational design, enabling him to uncover hidden talent and transform it into measurable impact. He is passionate about the human dynamics behind success, believing that the quiet, invisible contributors often hold the key to organisational excellence.

Beyond the boardroom, Mark is an avid mountaineer, drawn to the clarity, discipline, and resilience that come from scaling the world's most challenging peaks. He brings the same precision, courage, and focus to his work with organisations as he does to climbing mountains.

Through Finding the Hidden Talent, Mark shares the lessons, frameworks, and insights he has gathered over nearly four decades, helping leaders identify, nurture, and empower the people who genuinely make their organisations succeed.

www.ingramcontent.com/pod-product-compliance
Lightning Source LLC
Chambersburg PA
CBHW071438230926
51846CB00001B/271
9782746054844